Best wishes

Nobby Hill

NOBBY's
QUARTER MILE

The life story of Nobby Hills and the history of drag racing in his own words.

.... sometimes funny .... sometimes sad .... but never a drag....

Nobby Hills

NOBBY'S QUARTER MILE
by Nobby Hills

Published by
Dolphin Graphics
73 Doddshill Road
Dersingham
Kings Lynn Norfolk
PE31 6LP
Telephone: 01485 544596

First published 2008

Origination, design and print:
Dolphin Graphics
73 Doddshill Road
Dersingham
Kings Lynn Norfolk
PE31 6LP
Telephone: 01485 544596

ISBN
978-0-9559623-0-1

NOBBY'S QUARTER MILE

This book is dedicated to the memory

of Jodie Hills

One more angel in heaven

Inspirations

Inspirations

*A*fter reading Hot Rod Magazine about Drag Racing way back in 1958, I felt inspired to build and race dragsters, starting when it was a hobby orientated sport right through the decades, to when it became popular in this country.

I think and believe all drag racers are great people from the smallest of cars and bikes, all built on low budgets with much love and attention to detail, to the higher classed cars; I just loved them all.

Looking back over the years I can remember a time when Al O'Connor came with his Ford Pop Gasser down to run, everyone would stop what they were doing as well as me, it was just one of the many cars that I have witnessed over the years. Many other cars and teams always gained my attention The Stones with Gerry Andrews, DLT, Dave and Daddy Stone, to mention a few. Another car I remember well was the Jaguar altered named Paranoia, always impeccable and a pleasure to see go down the strip.

I built my latest car, Houndog 12, after surviving a most horrific accident whilst welding (when I almost met my maker) and then a very personal tragedy, the loss of my dearest first born daughter Jodie in a road accident. She was my number one fan as she had been brought up on the drag racing circuit and was very knowledgable and interested in it. This last Houndog car is a very special build (as Jodie was involved in it in every way with the car being built around her).

I feel I have reached a landmark, at 70 years old I can now recall the memories of how drag racing was, and the famous faces I have met along the way, and share my scrap book recollections to incorporate my life story along with the history of drag racing in this country.

This brilliant sport has possibly not been as popular as some but none the less an awful lot of fun and excitement can be had from it.

Nobby

Nobby Hills

Written with love from my wife Anne ... on life with Nobby

Well, we all now know my husband Nobby
has this all-consuming hobby.
He gives his all to the love of his life
and, sometimes, he even remembers his wife ...

No, seriously though, over the years,
we've had lots of fun and shed many tears.

When Santa Pod was our second home,
we always arrived like the 'Clampits',
the car in the trailer, the kids and toys,
the birds in a cage
and some more bits!

It was important for Nobby to have me involved,
and duly set me the task
of driving the crew truck at race events
(what a job for a mum, I ask!).
With our two little girls, I spent many an hour
in that truck, on the 'line'
watching that shower!

But couldn't have been more excited and prouder
when that car fired-up
and got louder and louder.

As the smoke cleared from
those fierce-some burnouts,
there appeared Nobby, directing the scene,
Stetson on head and waiting for green!
And what a crowd pleaser,
The Houndog Team.

NOBBY'S QUARTER MILE

Then, surprisingly so, it was all behind us,
but never the one to pine,
Nobby's passion for Country Music
Soon has us dancing in Line.
With Nobby ramrodding and Jodie teaching,
Katie 'dj'ing and me all-rounding,
the 'wheels' were turning again,
so any thoughts of a normal life
were clearly quite insane!

But time has a way of marching on
and we had to deal with our sorrow.
We take a deep breath and think of our love,
and try to look to tomorrow.

Well, what can I say about Nobby
he's certainly ONE OF KIND.
He's HONEST, STEADFAST and DECENT
and that's not just love being blind!

A man you can TRULY RELY ON
and know that his WORD IS HIS BOND.
He's the BEST HUSBAND and FATHER
and goes the full mile and beyond.

I love, respect and adore him
but there's one thing he just has to hate.
He always throws this at me,
The fact that I'm always late!

Getting back to that Houndog,
just seems he was having a nap.
It's been a long time and a lot of hard work
but he's finally closing the gap.
Of past achievements and what might be
He thinks to himself and decides.
It seems there's life in the old dog yet
and he'll soon be 'boiling them hides'!

Thanks ...

I would like to say a big thank you to everyone who has contributed towards this book, friends old and new, especially those who have added their memories and stories of me (good and bad!).

Also those who have let me use their photographs and have helped me remember dates.

Thanks also to my GP and to my surgeon and dentist and all medical staff who have kept me going and without whose skills I would not be here today.

It goes without saying, to my family, the greatest love of all.

Nobby

An introduction

Dave Lee Travis (DLT)

Nobby Hills – now that name suggests, either an as yet undiscovered part of the Lake district, or one of the most celebrated characters in Britain's drag racing fraternity – I can assure you it is the latter!!

We first met at a drag race dinner dance in Luton in 1970 where we struck up a friendship which has lasted right up to the present day.

It became apparent very quickly that Nobby not only had an incredible knowledge about the building and racing of these beasts but he was also a great guy to be around, always greeting everyone with a smile and generously sharing his vast knowledge with the people who took the trouble to ask for his advice.

I certainly benefited from Nobby's input when I first started getting serious about driving and my best run of 220 mph in 6.6 seconds might never have happened without his early involvement with "the Needle".

From my monkey bike through "Tender Trap" and on to that 2000 hp top fuel pulse racer I have great memories of my time with Nobby and Anne at the Pod.

Every sport has its heroes and being the guy he is made it a thrill for me to be asked to add just a few words at the beginning of his story which I know you will find fascinating.

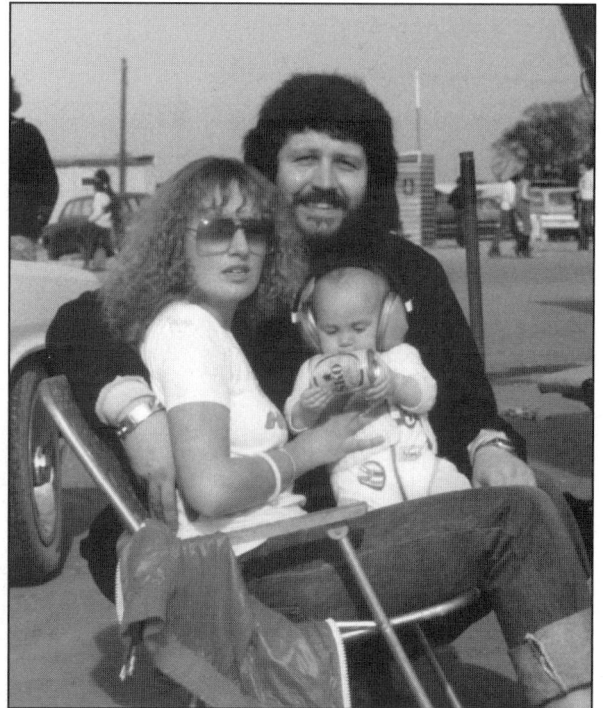

Dave, Anne and Jodie as a baby

Jodie Lou with DLT's headphones on

Nobby Hills

Having mentioned that Nobby has always been good enough to answer any questions thrown at him, the only one I haven't asked him is, "when are you going to slow down?"

I have a feeling it's going to be a long wait !!

Cheers Nobby

From your friend Dave Lee Travis.

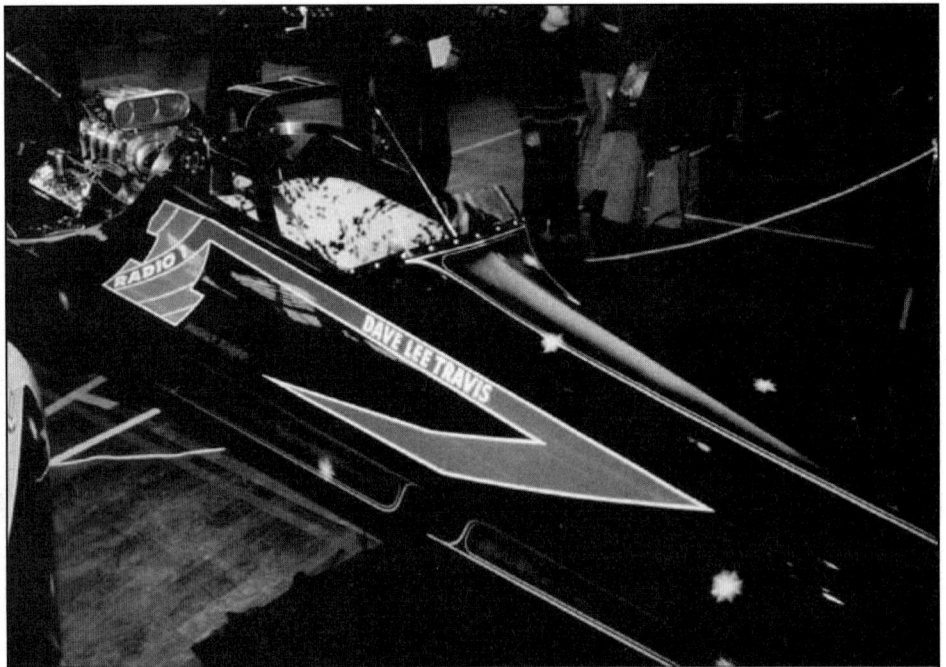

'The Needle' – top fuel dragster driven by DLT

Why drag racing?

How it began?

*T*o help understand Nobby's passion and enthusiasm ... first understand what Drag Racing is and means to so many people out there, young and old.

Drag Racing as we know it started way back in the mid forties in the USA, when the teenagers of the day started dropping the new post-war V8 engines into their early chassis and bodies. The basic idea was not new, as Ford's famous 'Flathead' V8 had been popular for the same purpose since the early thirties, but the new OHV engines now gave people a taste of power hitherto only equalled in racing cars.

Mike Hutcherson and Houndog 4 (right) against Clive Skilton

Naturally, when people start "hot rodding", or souping up their cars, it's not long before they want to start racing, and so the inevitable happened.

The first races were held on deserted highways, or even on the main "drag" through town – the American high street or main road. Thus "Drag Racing" became the name of the game. Next some of the more responsible racers got together with local police and civic officials and eventually drag strips began to open up on old airfields and wasteland, with the first organised meeting at Goleta, California in 1948, organised by the Santa Barbara Timing Association.

Slowly but surely the sport began to grow in popularity with clubs and strips opened up from coast to coast. In 1951 the National Hot Rod Association was formed with the founder members including one Wally Parks (Wally was still at the top of this, the biggest drag racing association in America until he sadly passed away in September 2007). With its popularity still rising, the times started to tumble, and by the mid fifties the top cars were turning in times of over 150mph in front of crowds reported as exceeding 10,000.

By 1964 a whole new world had opened up with the two biggest barriers broken by "Big Daddy" Don Garlits. The first run into the sevens and the second a terminal speed of over 200mph.

1964 also saw the N.H.R.A. introduce a new electronic start system, which became known as the "Christmas Tree"; and the first wheel-standing cars and factory experimental cars were seen. These FX cars were later to become the Funny Cars that are so loved today.

Most of this took place in the USA but in England

'hot rodding' also experienced a sharp rise to fame. It started with the formation of the British Hot Rod Association in 1959, although the first meeting did not occur until 1963 at Duxford. Following that things started to happen and 1964 and 1965 did see two visits by the American Drag Racing Team (read Nobby's experience!). Then in 1966 the biggest happening of all – on April 11th Santa Pod Raceway was opened up as Europe's first permanent drag racing strip and by 1970 the sport had progressed to hold its first international event there.

So what really makes this sport so great ...

Basically it is a race between two machines from a standing start for a distance of a quarter mile with the first to the finish taking the win and going forward to the next round. The machines are "staged" on the start line by photo-electric beams and when both competitors are ready to start the signal begins. This is in the form of a light countdown running amber, amber, green and on the green you go. Any machine that goes before the green is fouled out of the competition and this is shown by a red light (the evil eye) at the bottom of the "Christmas Tree" start system.

At the finish line there are more photo-electric beams which feed into a computer to determine the winner, using the time taken for each machine to actually cover the quarter mile (ET) and the terminal speed they cross the finish line (TS). The elapsed time is recorded to .001 and the terminal speed to 0.01mph.

Because of the vast difference in power put out by different cars they are put into different classes i.e. jets, rocket cars, out and out fuel dragsters

and funny cars.

Funny cars are popular and well known because of their unpredictable speed and WOW factor.

All in all an afternoon watching drag racing can be extremely exciting.

NOBBY'S QUARTER MILE

Dragster Fuel:

NITROMETHANE: CH_3NO_2

A member of the group of Organic Chemicals called Nitroparaffins.

The nitromethane molecule comprises 1 atom of carbon, 3 atoms of hydrogen, 1 atom of nitrogen, 2 atoms oxygen.

Nitromethane may be prepared by boiling an aqueous solution of sodium nitrite with a halo-geno-acetic acid.

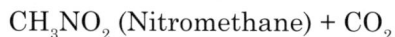

$NaNO_2 + CH_2Cl\, CO_2Na$ gives

$NaCl + [CH_2(NO_2)\, CO_2H]$ gives

CH_3NO_2 (Nitromethane) $+ CO_2$

Or by direct liquid or vapour phase Nitration

$CH_3\, CH_2\, CH_3$ reacted with Nitric Acid @ 400°C gives

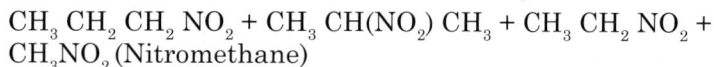

$CH_3\, CH_2\, CH_2\, NO_2 + CH_3\, CH(NO_2)\, CH_3 + CH_3\, CH_2\, NO_2 + CH_3NO_2$ (Nitromethane)

Dragster Fuel:

METHANOL: CH_3OH

A member of the group of Organic Chemicals called Alcohols.

The methanol molecule comprises 1 atom of carbon, 4 atoms of hydrogen, 1 atom oxygen.

Methanol may be prepared from water-gas and hydrogen by a hydrogenation process at 20 atmospheres pressure, passed though a catalyst of copper zinc and chromium oxides @ 300°C.

$CO + 2H_2$ ---> CH_3OH (Methanol)

Or by catalytic oxidation of methane, with oxygen at 100 atmospheres within a copper tube @ 200°C

$2CH_4 + O_2$ ---> CH_3OH (Methanol)

Page 15

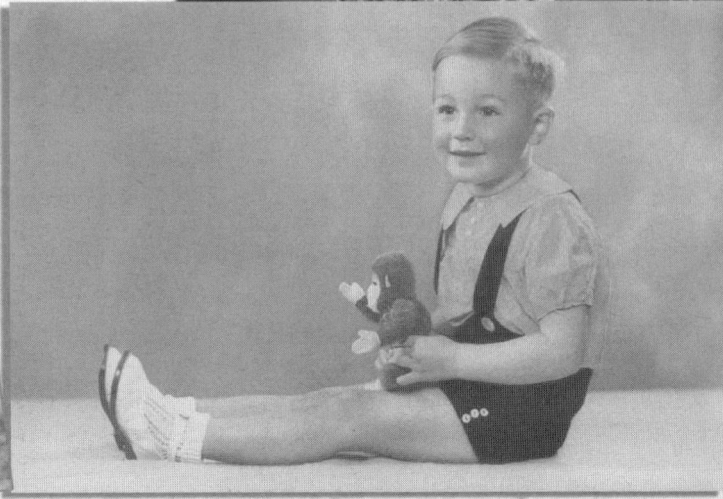

Friday 13th November 1936 ...

Born to Thomas Edward and Jessie Isabel: a son weighing 10lbs named Norman Thomas Hills

This large bundle of joy was to become known as Nobby Hills – drag racer, easily recognisable by his tall frame, stetson (sometimes flip flops) and cowboy boots.

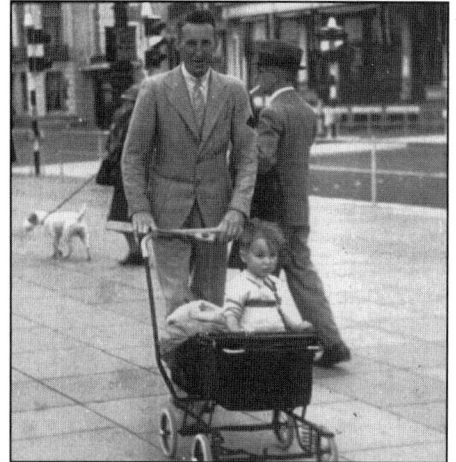

Nobby in his pram being pushed by his father

In 1962, in just eight months, Nobby with the help of Les Hill, George Myring, Ron Doyle and Colin Holloran, in their spare time at Jack Oldings factory at Hatfield built, from American designs around a blown 3.4 litre Jaguar engine, Morris commercial rear axle, Mark 7 gearbox and Ford Popular front axle. It ran originally on Methanol with 10-12 lb blower boost this was to become Nobby's famous Houndog 1.

This led to Nobby competing at the first British Drag Festival in 1964 with Houndog 1 being designated dragster number 72. From then on drag racing became a very important part of his life ....

Read on to hear what Nobby has to say with his memories and recollections and his vast array of photographic memorabilia.

*Podington then
and how it is today*

Podington 1930s

A Dragstrip in the making

Podington was a small picturesque English village situated in the heart of Bedfordshire. This sleepy quiet village's life was to change forever. In the late 1930s with the outbreak of World War II plans were made to build an airfield on the surrounding farmland close to the village.

Work started in September 1940. I was four years old at the time and lived in Ware in Hertfordshire not knowing what the impact of this location would have on the rest of my life.

By 1943 the 92nd Bombardment Group were an operational unit at the new airfield flying their B17s. This meant a drastic change for all the local people, the once quiet village was suddenly populated with many American servicemen. They outnumbered the locals about by 100 to 1! The Americans turned out to be polite and much appreciated by the villagers proving generous to all who met them; remember we were all on very tight rations. Village life carried on in as normal a way as possible with the constant drone of the B17s leaving the airfield and returning after many a dangerous mission. Sadly many airmen lost their lives at this time.

Although these were not happy times for everybody involved, the airmen tried to bring some of the American happiness to the small village of Podington, often seen cycling to the local village hall to arrange for supplies to be available for the village dances. On the base, some famous American heroes of the time visited. One such man was the much revered Glen Miller whose sound will always remind us of the American presence surrounding the village.

Many aircrew passed through this airfield and several left their mark including the arrival of the American actor James Cagney to open a bar which would be known as the "Cagney Cellar". Bob Hope was also one of the famous visitors. Many paintings were left on barrack walls and billets. One such piece of art has now been dismantled and reassembled at the American Duxford War Museum near Cambridge.

One of the worst disasters to hit the base was on 20th May 1944 when three B17s crashed on the same day. One crashed on takeoff overshooting the runway and two others collided as one was coming into land. With great sadness all 21 airmen lost their lives on that day.

The security and operations of the airfield were always helped and maintained by the Podington Home Guard. The Home Guard were always on duty when the returning B17s came back from bombing raids. If there were wounded on these flights they would fire flares to make sure the ambulances were there by the runway to get immediate assistance to the injured crew. Perhaps these were the B17s that I would see coming back from raids in Germany and other mainland European locations as a child on my grandfather's farm, who knows?

In 1944 the 92nd Bombardment Group left nearly as quickly as they came, everything literally disappeared as they moved on to Listris in France. If only I had known at my young age how this empty airfield was later on to become the great Santa Pod Raceway.

Lt Harry S Culver.

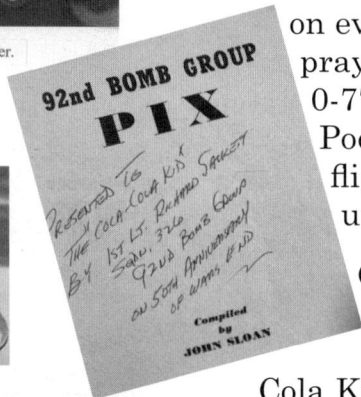

92nd BOMB GROUP
PIX

Presented To
The "Coca-Cola Kid"
By 1st Lt. Richard Sackett
Sqd. 326
92nd Bomb Group
on 50th Anniversary
of Wars End

Compiled by
JOHN SLOAN

My Crew

BACK ROW LEFT TO RIGHT:
BERNIE DeVORE – ENGINEER   From NEBRASKA   FRONT Row:
DOM TAURONE – CO-PILOT   JOE TRIPLETT W...
HERB WOLINSKY – NAVIGATOR   BOSTON MASS.   FROM NEW Y...
DAVE HAUER – PILOT   NEW YORK   NORT FOLK ARK...
PAUL GOODMAN – BOMBARDIER   MICHIGAN   GLENN E. BOL...
CLYDE ANGLE – TAIL GUNNER   FROM...

With so many Americans in the area many characters were remembered. One of the main names that kept re-occurring was a man called "Pinky" Biggeris, a dab hand at dance organisation. Pinky never forgot this place or the friends he lost and made, both American and English. In 1978 "Pinky" appeared at Podington dressed as Santa Claus. He headed for the local vicarage and supplied many presents for the local children. Much to the surprise of the Vicar and much to Pinky's surprise his thoughts of that lonely airfield were now filled with the enjoyment of youngsters chasing their dreams of speed. The sound of the much heard B17 engines had been replaced with the harsh sound of blown nitro engines.

During my research for this book, I have been entrusted with a B4 flight bag and the hat worn on every flight made and the new testament prayer book of Captain Harry S. Culver 0-771619. He flew on 33 missions from Podington airfield, so I am sure if this flight bag could speak it could tell some unbelievable stories.

One story told by Harry, first hand to a new and very good friend of mine Gerry Darnell, who was nicknamed the "Coca Cola Kid" by American servicemen, due to the fact that as a small child at the time he was always asking for a drink of coca cola which he developed quite a liking for.

Gerry eventually went on to work with his brother at Podington airfield during the war and was told Harry's ship had been badly damaged. In his own words Harry said: "a lesser pilot would have gone down, but I worked out how the flak was coming up one left side one right, so I manoeuvred the

NOBBY'S QUARTER MILE

B17 right when it came up left and left when it came up right and never got another hit and got the plane back to Podington". He had this flight bag with him then and had become a great friend of Gerry's.

Another of Harry's stories: one foggy morning on 'take off' Bill Brockmyers B17 had crashed in Hayes Wood. Harry was on his take off run and in his words he said to me all these years later that this was his one and only mistake during his service of being a pilot, rather than take off on instruments he took off visually. The fog was really thick and was freezing on the windscreens, he knew he was getting near to the end of the runway, (now the drag strip) again he told me, "I just could not see nothing – the speed told me that I must go, there was no return, I pulled the stick back, we lifted off, we heard the trees brushing on the B17, but we kept going, and eventually broke into sunshine", my co pilot turned to me and shook my hand, and said "Harry, you're the best!" We had a successful trip.

Sadly Harry died of Parkinsons disease two years ago.

I think as time has passed by I realise now how dreadful those early war years were at Podington with the terrible loss of young lives. I understand that there were 374 air and ground crew lost.

After the 92nd Squadron, in the middle to late 1950's, The North London and Mid Bucks Car Club used to run small club meetings using part of the perimeter and the smaller cross runway for circuit racing. This was organised by Pat Eason and his father The airfield was also used occasionally by the National Sprint Association.

Nobby holding the flight bag and the prayer book above

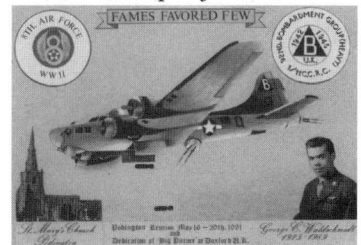

I feel we must never forget the others who died in the war as this poem written by a friend of mine expresses.

Remembering –

Each year we all remember

Those who fought for us and died,

Also mothers, wives and daughters

Who stayed at home and cried.

We can't begin to know the feelings

Of all of those who fought,

The fear and terror of not knowing

If friends were killed or caught.

Those who were lucky to come home

Hope it would never happen again,

Unfortunately war still goes on today

They must have thought they fought in vain.

Old veterans with medals stand proudly

As they lay wreaths of poppies red,

To honour those brave men and boys

Who had to fight and now are dead.

And so as we remember

We bow our heads and pray,

Pray for our families and our loved ones

And for peace in our world one day.

Diane King

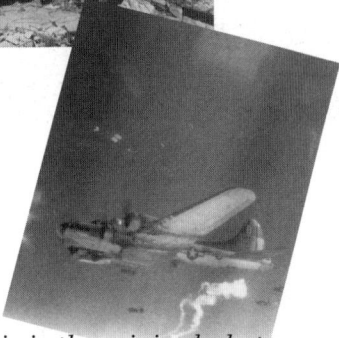

This is the original photo of the B17 on the wall of Duxford which the artist copied.

War memories as a youngster ...

V1 Doodlebug Rocket crashes out of the sky

I have many memories of my school holidays but even today I can vividly remember spending my weekends and school holidays on my grandfather's farm at Much Hadham. He had two cars, a Vauxhall 21 and a Morris Cowley with a vertical split screen and a Fordson tractor running on paraffin and starting on petrol. My cousin John also had an Austin Ruby. At a very young age I was encouraged to drive a four wheel cart which in a way was good because the cart horses were very obedient. I can remember being able to go wide on tight corners on the farm and getting the work cart through the gap. I also remember driving the tractor, with the brake and the clutch on the same pedal. My cousin used to let me drive this around the fields. When I came to a gate I had to stand on the clutch and brake pedal with both feet and pull myself up with the steering wheel because I was not heavy enough to operate it normally.

My grandad's farm was very close to Hunsdon Airfield where Spitfires were based and very often these pilots, during their test flight would fly over the farm very low and they would wave to my cousin and I. I could see their faces, with their leather headgear and sometimes they would come round again and dip their wings.

One moment which I recall when I was walking towards the farm through a neighbours field I heard a V1 coming. I knew what it was because of the distinguishing sound of the motor. I also knew that if the motor stopped there was every chance that it would nose dive. Immediately I broke into a panic run towards the farm as the rocket motor STOPPED! Within a few seconds there was a terrific explosion and blast, this thing had come down around 100 yards from where I was. The only damage was a destroyed haystack. When I had gathered my thoughts I went back to the crash site where everything was smoking. I retrieved a bent piece of the body about 6 inches square and about one eighth of an inch thick. I can still remember the warmth of the metal in my hand as the village bobby arrived and he said it was alright and I could take this piece home, which I did.

One of my fondest memories of my grandad on the farm was when I was about seven years old. I remember he always smoked white clay pipes for work, and I used to creep up on him when he was doing the milking or working on something and knock the pipe out of his mouth, nearly always making them break.

One day I crept up but he saw me coming, he said "what do you think you're going to do now?" I'm not sure what I said but he went on, "I am going to find out how clever you are, can you say your alphabet?" I said yes. He said go on then, which I did. He then said good, now what I want you to do is to say it backwards, he then proceeded to do just that, really quickly. Grandad then said if you learn to say it backwards I will give you half a crown (two shillings and six pence). That was a lot of money back in 1943 so three weeks later after much repetition I had this word perfect and showed him that I could do it, he immediately gave me my half a crown and said very good. I must confess from that day on I never knocked his clay pipe out of his mouth again and believe it or not I can still say the alphabet backward in less than 8 seconds!

When not on the farm I attended school at Ware. I had started school in 1941 at the age of five at St. Mary's infant school. I learnt to add up and write using a small blackboard and soft white chalk and a rubber (no pens and paper in those days). Some of the teachers I was pretty scared of. The uniform, if you can call it that, consisted of hob nail boots, long wool socks, short trousers, a lumber jacket and a 'Jacky Coogan' style cap. The school was divided into two halves, one for the infants and one for the juniors.

When the sirens sounded if I was at school all the classes were ushered as quickly as possible down the air-raid shelters that were located in the school gardens. I can remember about 300 of us children singing songs like, "you are my sunshine' and 'pistol packing mama' to help keep us cheerful and pass the time and to stop us being frightened as it was a rather frightening experience.

I progressed up into the juniors after two years at the infant part of the school. I preferred the junior school because I was able to take part in athletics and football and was made school captain and head boy at this school. I stayed there until aged eleven when I went on to Ware Secondary school. Here I was house leader (Shackleton Blue) and also school captain of sports, football and swimming. I obtained many medals and certificates for these subjects.

When not at school I often helped my mother

During these years Pill Boxes were on nearly every road in the South and East of England

with the groceries which came to a grand total of 25 shillings per week. (£1 and 30 new pence!). I remember how well my mum had coped during the war years with rationing. I can recall walking to school one day with my friend who was very excited about a pudding sweet he was going to have for the first time of his life for lunch. He said "my mum bought some rice today and we are going to have some rice pudding". I was quite surprised and told him we had rice pudding at least once a week as my mum always cooked it for us. What I had not realised was that my mum had bought and stored packets of rice before the outbreak of war and used a little of these every week. She did really well as with small helpings it lasted us throughout the war years. Another thing I remember was that in 1945 I saw and tasted my first banana, it seems really strange that up until then I had never encountered fruit grown in other countries.

In those days we did not have electricity but gas lights in our home and in the streets. I can still remember the man coming along with a great big rod to light the gas lights. A bit different to the instant lighting of today.

Often in Ware I remember the German bombers coming over and when I saw the markings I was pretty scared. I also remember watching the home guards training, using broomsticks because there was a shortage of 303 rifles.

The Super Fortress was something that I recall in those days when they were coming back from what I know now to be the bombing raids in Germany. I could always see that they were damaged with maybe only one or two props turning. I am now convinced that some of these could have well

been returning to Poddington Airfield which was nearby.

I also remember the Dakotas towing the gliders to Arnhem, sometimes there appeared to be hundreds of them, one after the other. I remember watching when one of the ropes came adrift and a glider went into a steep dive but then it levelled out landing about two miles away from where I stood. I promptly got on my bicycle and went to see for myself where it had landed in a field at Thunderidge. I even saw the troops gathered up and get into a truck I guess they went back and had another trip.

During the war, one time of the year, I always looked forward to, was when the potatoes on the local farm were ready for harvesting. This was "spud bashing" time. Most of the older kids from about ten years and above would volunteer for this. We would go to the farm on our bikes and would work from 8am to 6pm until all the spuds were removed from the fields and we received a little cash for this work which made for wonderful times.

Because of the war years I often went to stay with my dad's sister, my aunt who lived in Brighton. The beach at Brighton at this time was literally covered in mines washed up from the sea. One morning my dad and I were walking along the seafront, probably Madeira Drive. I remember to my dad's astonishment there were two or three young boys and girls, probably twelve or thirteen years old, that were running along the beach jumping on and off these mines, they were quite large, possibly two foot in diameter. Once dad realised we left rather quickly in case we got blown up.

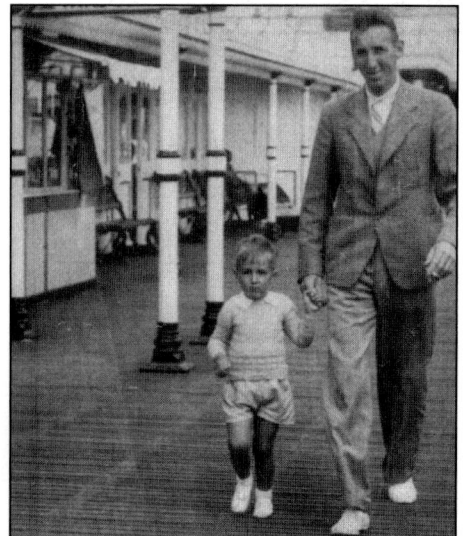

It was then that my love of country music was born. Often in my school lunch time as I got older I used to spend hours standing outside the Star Pub which the US GI's used in Ware. If I was lucky my patience would be rewarded with the sound of Hank Williams playing on the pub's jukebox. So began a life long affair with country music which I passed on to my family in later years.

1946 ...

The first television at Gamages in London and new arrivals – a double event!

I can still remember being taken by my father as a treat, when I was nine years old, to a very posh department store in Holborn, London called Gamages where they were showing the new *'in thing'*. It was a nine inch wide black and white television screen. I was very excited and fascinated by this. Things have certainly moved on today but to me that day still holds very special memories.

I have fond memories of listening to the radio and programmes such as Workers Playtime, Wilfred Pickles (Give'em the money Barney), Big Bill Campbell (Rocky Mountain Rhythm) and Norman Harper the yodelling cowboy who I saw at Finsbury Park Empire.

It was also at this time that I remember a surprise event, for me anyway in our family. The doctor was round and he asked me to look upstairs in the baby cot in my mother's bedroom, he said "take a look at this end", and I saw a small wrinkled up face, then he said, "look the other end". Instead of seeing a pair of feet there was another small wrinkled up face exactly the same, it was his little jokey way of introducing me to my new twin brothers, who were named Pat and John. Being a nine year old boy, I must admit I was much more taken with my visit to see the television! No offence to my twin brothers whom I preferred when they were a bit older!

Early television, mother and the twins, Nobby and the twins

Why did I become interested in building race cars?

This began when I was about ten years old, when boys of that age developed a liking for a trolley or a cart made from wood and used pram or pushchair wheels and axles. After a few trial cars I quickly realised that the faster ones were those boys that were lucky enough to have been given wheels that contained ball bearings. I looked around and eventually found, at the local dump (as one did in those days!), a set of four from a large pram. These had bearing wheels and also another major advantage being that they were of a larger diameter. So even at this age I had a real liking for speed.

With my basic layout on my cart vehicle I soon became the fastest in my street where I lived; its 30 yard short slopes were perfect for me. But after a week or so it became apparent to me that I could improve my beloved machine much more by the addition of a brake and even a steering wheel. This caused me to think hard for about an hour or so.

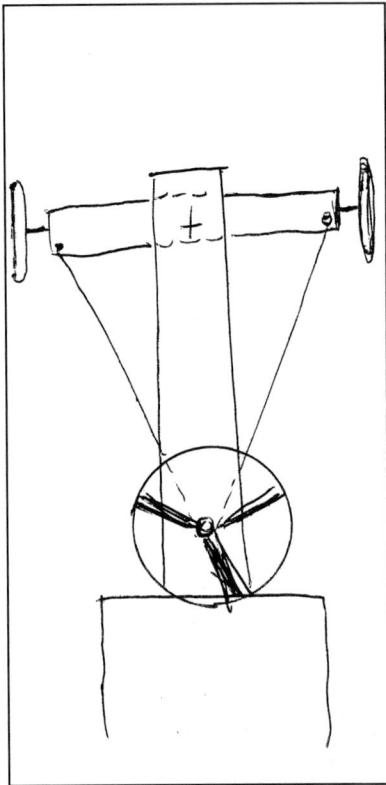

Early sketches of Nobby's

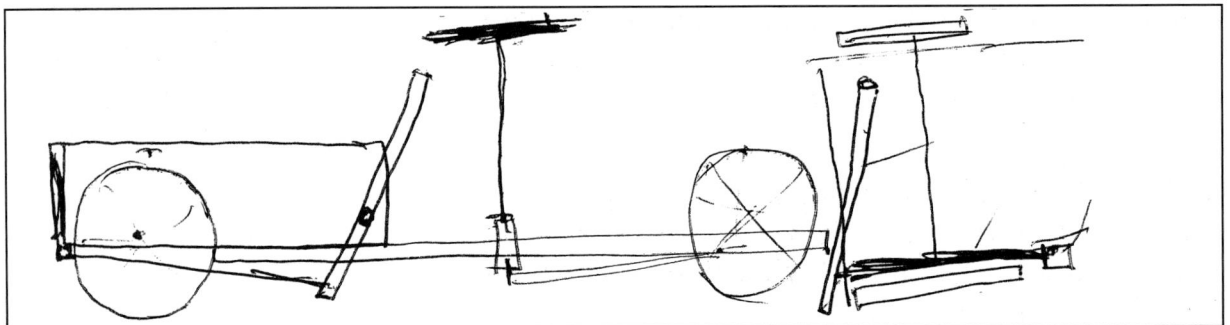

NOBBY'S QUARTER MILE

I took to my dad's garden shed, where there were a few hand tools and a drill bit. I soon discovered the latter was not suitable when mixing wood and metal, so my good friend's dad who worked in engineering, helped me by obtaining a steel drill bit to get the job done. Before I knew it I had thought up a steering mechanism totally on my own and it actually worked.

I had given this lots of thought and have included some of my old sketches to show just how mechanically minded I was.

So with an old car steering wheel and a piece of three quarter steel conduit, I crudely made my first dragster!!!

As I had progressed to senior school my interest in football and sports also continued and I played for the county schoolboys. Whilst at school I did not achieve particularly good marks as a scholar but I nearly always had the best marks in practical subjects which was always a help in my special car and bike projects. I was also allowed to use the school facilities and learnt woodwork and metal work.

I modified and built myself a speedway cycle and went to the local track at Rye House to have a try out. At this time my dad used to take me to Harringay stadium where I remember seeing people like Vic and Ray Dugan, Split Waterman and a local man from Ware Stan Bedford – I guess I was leaning towards motorsports.

I remember well my speedway cycle mechanical project which lead towards competitive speed and especially the wooden ramp which I made up and lined up nine of my chums laying side by side then I used to jump over them!

1947–1953 ...

The motor bike I did not have! and starting work

I spent a lot of time being interested in motor bikes. I used to go every time I could to watch the scrambling at Danbridge in Much Hadham. I just had to listen to the 500cc BSA and Matchless – a real sound.

I pestered my dad but he just would not let me consider buying one. I think he must have dismounted the wrong way on the one he owned in his younger days.

I carried on dreaming for the next few years but money was scarce and he still said no. So I carried on learning my welding fabrication curve, mixed with army cadets, swimming and athletics and football. So life was hard but possibly not boring; but no motorbike for me just a distant dream as many a boy had.

When I was fifteen I finished my education without any qualifications and as my father had worked at Allen & Hamburys as Chief Security Officer (now Glaxo) he was able to get me a job as a Laboratory Assistant in the N10 Research Laboratory. This was not what I wanted to do but I guess it was a start. After ten months I found a job in an engineering sheet metal work company as a trainee gas welder. I loved this job and I soon learnt to gas weld, silver soldering and brazing.

The first Christmas party was quite an event to remember as whilst we were preparing for it I had a very scary moment. One of the lads had purchased some large balloons, we were all blowing them up and decorating the workshop. This took quite some time to do. One of the lads, to be annoying kept going around and bursting our balloons with a cigarette. We had a Canadian guy working with us at the time, he got rather annoyed with this and turned and said to me, "I'll soon put a stop to that"! With this he disappeared into the welding area, on his return in his hand was a fully inflated balloon. He said to me "hang this one up boy", to which I duly obeyed.

Enjoying my work

We looked around to make sure all the balloons were in place. The Canadian guy said to me, "here he comes", referring to our annoying mate, with this true to form, he put the end of his cigarette to the last balloon I had hung up. To my amazement and total shock it exploded into a ball of fire engulfing the cigarette man's head. I was absolutely shocked, I looked at my Canadian friend who was nearly falling off his chair with laughter, then quickly looked over at our cigarette man, burnt eyebrows, hairline reduced by an inch and the blackest face you have ever seen. The Canadian guy said, he won't be spoiling our Christmas party again! That was my introduction to the dangers of acetylene gas.

I left this job when I was sixteen and moved to another local company where I could learn electric arc welding. I was always the assistant to one chap, he was a person I had known all my life and lived about fifty yards up the road from myself, he too was a keen footballer – he was known as Mr. "Specky" Chappel. There was very little Specky did not know about metal fabrication, welding and blacksmithing. He taught me so much and without his input I would have been a much less qualified

Nobby and Specky at work

fitter/welder and very unlikely to have achieved 27 years of management in the heavy construction equipment and manufacturing industry. I stayed at this job learning a lot until I had to leave to do my National Service.

This company used to manufacture lamp posts for street lighting. The week I started there they were awarded a contract to manufacture and install the very first floodlights for Tottenham Football Club. I could not believe my luck, my football idle at the time was Spurs goalkeeper Ted Ditchburn, I used to go to White Hart Lane whenever I could and watch him from behind the goal. So to think there would be a chance that when the floodlights were installed during the summer months that I might see him in the grounds certainly inspired me to work on this job.

We started work at the Spurs ground under the grandstand making the steel moulds for the concrete posts that would hold the cluster of lights, one in each corner of the stadium. Once the reinforced steel was put in they were then filled with concrete. If I remember right, when they were complete they weighed in at around 4½ tons and were 70 feet long.

I began to wonder how they would make the journey from under the stand to the four corners of the ground. I asked Specky who told me not to worry as Jack Collings the Steeplejack was going to supervise and erect them in position. This was a fantastic experience, this man was a genius, he achieved this job with a 25 ton hand winch, rollers, planks, sheets of wood, guide ropes and a 30 ft 18 inch sphere stick which we fabricated. Unfortunately it was not possible to get any heavy equipment into the football ground.

After a few weeks I told Specky how clever I thought he was. He told me one of the odd jobs that he was responsible for during the war years. He said that sometimes after the dogfights and shooting over London, there may be 16mm cannon holes in the gasometers.

He proceeded to tell me how he would take a welding generator and weld them up to stop the leaks. I could not believe this (as they were filled with gas), until he explained how it was so very simple and clever. I know it's hard to believe but true, he would have some ¼ inch thick steel plates (about 8 inches in diameter) and formed like a teacup saucer. He then took some special clay that he would mould and form into an o-ring 6 inches in diameter, which was then put round the cannon hole. With the arc welder set up and ready he would then put the saucer over the hole and the clay o-ring, kneel on it to seal the gas leak, and then arc weld it up, he said the consistency of the clay is most important. Yes Sir, I believe that!

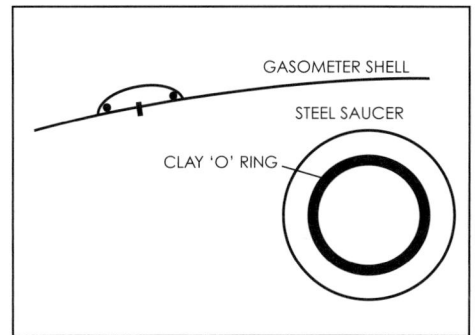

I enjoyed reading and round about 1950 I started to get interested in drag racing after seeing a picture of Don Garlits car in a magazine.

Nobby smartly dressed in uniform

1955-1956 ...

National Service and country sounds

The learning curve continued but with the addition of girls, beer and cigarettes. During this period always at the back of my mind was National Service.

Yes, it arrived I did my basic training at Oswestry and Rhyll in Wales, I was then posted to 22 Light AA Regiment in West Germany. The winter training in Winterburge, West Germany where we had to drain trucks of antifreeze which froze solid with midday temperatures of 17° below zero. We were in tents with oil stoves; even butter froze. It was terrible up there at that time, with the cold as I had never known before. It was so intense with up to four feet of snow and ten of us shared a tent with five paraffin stoves going. When we woke up in the morning there was half an inch of ice hanging inside the tent!

In June 1955 I joined the RA and spent two years stationed at Menden, West Germany. As I was into Country Music, this was great for me with three or four country radio shows a day – American Forces Network and in 1956 I heard the King Elvis Presley for the very first time. (I forgot to remember to forget you).

Whilst in the RA in Germany (22LAA), after arriving at Mendon, West Germany I very quickly had to take another driving test. This was because I was driving a right hand drive vehicle on the right hand side of the road.

The day arrived to take my test, so I reported to

a Second Lieutenant who was with a seven ton truck. No problem I thought, this was the same model truck that I had taken my first test in when in the UK.

He was quite a friendly person, so off we went, we drove around the town for some time, he asked me about the road signs, then we drove off into the countryside and onto smaller roads. After about twenty minutes we were on a fairly straight road which was just about wide enough for two vehicles to pass. He then asked me to turn around and go back the way we had come.

I knew he wanted me to do a three point turn staying on the road. I drove on for about another mile, he commented, "in your own time Hills". By this time I had spotted a small farm with a yard coming up on the right hand side of the road. I felt there was just enough room to get around without stopping! I proceeded to turn into the farmyard and yes I just made it, I turned around without stopping and proceeded back down the road, the opposite way to which we had come. I continued to drive, his comments were, "that's not quite what I wanted Hills, I was hoping you would turn on the road but I'll give you full marks for initiative, you pass, let's go back to the base".

My service life carried on as normal until two weeks later when I was told to report to our HQ to continue my driving career, here I was given duties which made my life a lot easier. These duties were now to drive Officers wives to the shops, their children to school and Officers and their wives to parties in the evenings. All this in my VW bus!

On one of my usual week day shopping trips with the Officers wives, it was late afternoon and the

Adjutant's wife was the last drop at her home after shopping. I was the driver as per usual of the six seater VW bus, as I backed into the driveway of her house I noticed she was sitting in the middle of the bus, next to the sliding side door. I made a move to get out and go round to open the sliding door but she called out not to bother, she said, "I think this will be more enjoyable", with that she leaned over and dropped all her shopping in the front seat, to my absolute amazement and horror as a Private in the army and the boss's wife about to do what I thought! I was only eighteen and she was about thirty five years old. She speedily pulled her skirt waist high, I couldn't believe my eyes, heels, stockings and suspenders and she was a very attractive lady at that. Then to make matters worse she was in no hurry to let the skirt down. Remember, I was only about six months into my National Service and was very much a male! I dare not say or do a thing as if I did I knew it would be the quickest way to end my National Service in a cell for six months. So unfortunately no boy changed into a man that day. But how I remember it well and I must admit on future shopping trips with the wives when she came along I made sure she was the last drop off and she always climbed over the seat and into the front. A real good show!

Within eight months of my driving duties I ended up as the Commanding Officer's Chauffeur. This was much better for me as I was allowed to wear shoes and no army belt!

One of my great pals in the army was Ron Bashford he was in the Troop with me and we would do all the guard duties on Christmas Eve. But this particular time in 1956, we were both given the time off so we decided to go to the local bars in town as per usual. Both being young, we had too much to drink. I helped Ron walk home and when we got to the guard house one of our lads was in the sentry box outside, so I went over and said would he let Ron stand behind the box while I go and book us both in. I then attempted to approach the guardroom door and to my amazement the Provost Sergeant was at the desk in his white webbing, belt and gaiters. I closed the door, went into the Guard Room and said "Hills and Bashford sober and properly dressed" as I could just about manage this without a slur. He said "never, where's that bloody Bashford?" Next, the guard room door flew open, which was about three inches thick, nearly knocking me over, and in came Ron, hitting the edge of the table, knocking the Provost Sergeant backwards off his chair! I stood there looking on in amazement; all we could see was boots, legs in the air on the other side of the table. His sharp white cap was sliding down the floor. This of course led to us spending the next two days locked up and we were charged with being drunk and disorderly and then we got seven days confined to barracks unfortunately.

Whilst I had many happy and fun times I would have loved to have been at home in Ware. I made the best of these times as you do and made many close pals. Most of my friends were ambulance drivers and small car drivers. We were always meeting up outside at the various parties and regular events which we took the Officers to.

Alongside my driving duties I had to complete my normal Forces training. This included learning to handle rifles, stengun and bren guns on the ranges. This I really enjoyed and turned out to be quite a good shot. This is pretty much how I spent the two years required of me at the time.

Probably one of the my longest lasting memories are of the radio stations playing the fantastic country sounds and my discovery of Elvis to which my cars were named after his hit "Houndog".

At the end of 1956 the Twenty Second Light AA Regiment (my regiment) was moving to Cyprus, I figured this was the time to put in for my fourteen days leave, before we left.

Sadly I never did get to Cyprus as after my leave they told me they had enough men to go there and so I was posted back to Germany into another AA Regiment with a dozen or so other Gunners from my original regiment.

I was not too concerned as I thought someone with my driving experience would be offered a similar job with the new Regiment but how wrong can a man be.

I remember the first morning on parade, there were about four of us in Troop F from the previous twenty second AA Regiment. The Parade Sergeant was slight and skinny and very loud. One of the lads that came along with me noted that unlike our old regiment none of the NCOs had any ribbons on their uniforms.

Eventually the Sergeant got round to us new troops, we were all a little long haired compared to the new gunners and not quite so skinny. His loud words were to us, "what sort of Regiment have you lot come from?"

The guy who noted the lack of ribbons, promptly replied, "a real regiment where the NCOs had medals and ribbons". He was immediately put on a charge with three days confined to barracks.

From then on we took it in turns to see the Company Sergeant Major, as my turn came I walked in and stood to attention and said, "368 Gunner Hills, Sir". He said to me, "you are a B4 driver". Thinking to myself this is where it all gets better, and explained what I had been doing as a driver in the last eighteen months; he said, "well Hills, that's great, but we will be teaching you warfare, not the welfare of the mothers and you will be driving a gun tractor. Report to Bombardier Robertson", which I did.

It was a very young Regiment and I remember there were eight gun tractors in our troop. In a short space of time I was asked to park all the gun tractors in the large garages, this was a little difficult because the guns were four wheeled and the unit length was about 60 feet. But this job did get me away from the other boring chores.

There were many operations in my time with this Regiment. One I can remember, there were forty eight trucks and trailers in the Regiment and I was the only one able to manoeuvre my truck and trailer off the road into the woods without unhitching the four wheeled gun (which was 60 feet long!) This was quite a nightmare for a mere eighteen year old. The Adjutant was quite proud of me and came round a couple of nights later with a bottle of German beer to reward me for my good driving, which was rather thoughtful.

I also rode motor bikes whilst in the services and one of our games was riding at 60 mph directly towards a ten foot concrete wall, usually there would be about eight of us trying this and the winner would be the one that left the shortest skid mark on the tar mac. I never did win this but it was such good fun!

One very harrowing memory I did have whilst in Germany was my visit to the Concentration Camp at Bergen Belson in North Germany, where Anne Frank died; it was a very sad and humbling place. Conditions in this camp were so terrible that nearly half of the camp's population died of disease, starvation, exposure, exhaustion, brutal beatings and the awful gas chambers. Most of the buildings had to be burned down but I did see part of the gas chambers, horrible pictures and mass graves that read *"Here lies 2,500"*. I found it was a very sad, quiet and eerie place, with an indescribable smell; one could not help thinking of all those innocent, poor people who lost their lives. It is hard to envisage how something like that could have happened and how horrible people can be to each other. I know we all felt the same and on the way back to the barracks we stopped for a beer about eight miles away. When we spoke to the people in the cafe of our visit they said they could smell Belson camp sometimes, when it was operating, depending on the wind, even at that distance, which was naturally quite distressing for them. I think at that moment we all wanted to ensure peace in our world and no more wars for the future.

I also visited the Mohne and Eider dams. Like the Mohne, the Eider dam was a gravity dam made from granite masonry blocks built between 1908 and 1914. It is located 60 miles south east of the Mohne. The Eider dam we were told held back 200 million tons of water – making it the largest reservoir in Germany. These were the targets of the famous Dambuster Squadron, whose daring

Postcard Nobby sent home to his mother

raid on these incredibly large reservoirs were perhaps one of the most incredible and well planned raids of the Second World War which are still remembered today.

Time did however in the main, pass quickly and I was now looking at two months before the end of my soldiering, those last months did pass slowly and in June 1957 I was discharged; an interesting time I think.

So it was back to my home in Ware and returning to my old job making moulds for lamp posts.

Postcard Nobby sent home to his mother

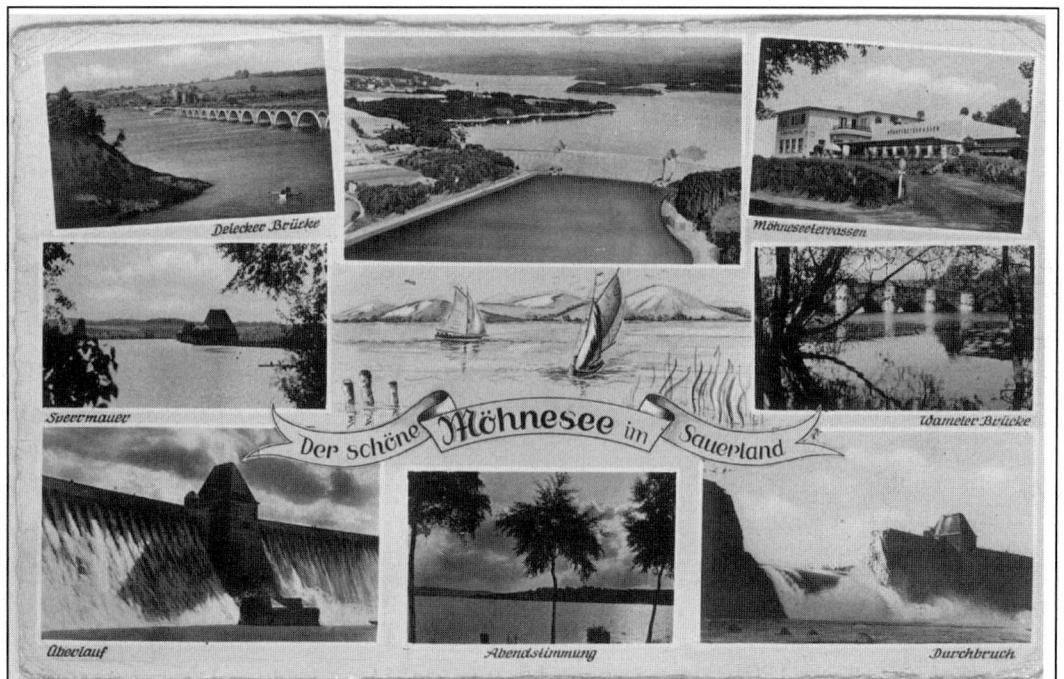

1957 ...

My first car

Icame out of the Forces in 1957 and whatever happened I just had to get a car, a real car that is. I was able to borrow twenty five pounds from my dad and I purchased my first car, a 1935 Chrysler Windsor. It was a straight six with less than 3,000cc but for the year it was good, with a factory fitted radio and overdrive.

I then realised that if I was out and about and it would not go I would not know how to fix it. So over the next few months I tackled all sorts of

Fond memories

mechanically minded people and with a thirst for knowledge of the workings of the engine I read books. All I knew was, I needed to know.

Tax was twelve pounds per year, the insurance was twelve pounds and ten shillings and petrol was only three shillings and four pence per gallon. (thirty two new pence!)

One little problem I encountered was that the starter ring gear came off the fly wheel. Everyone was worried, "that's its day", they said. I couldn't see their problem, I carefully prised the ring gear back and welded it in about six places through the starter motor location with cast iron nickel electrodes. I ran this car for two years without a problem and sold it on for twelve pounds (registration number DBH44) – I wish I still had it. Also at this time I enjoyed reading the Hot Rod Magazine which fired me up no end and gave me lots of ideas ....

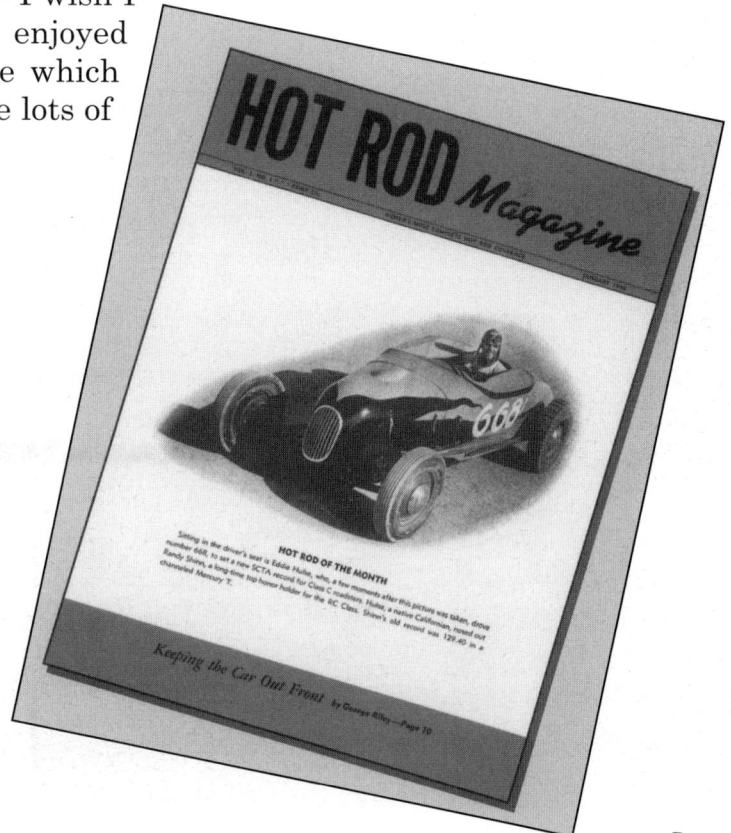

1958-1960 ...

To build a dragster

My next car was a DeSoto 1958 Fireflite 331 Hemi. I only kept it for a few months, I was looking very closely at drag racing hot rods by then so I purchased a MK1 Zodiac. It as a lovely car, probably okay for pulling a trailer.

After completing my National Service I again worked at my job making moulds for lampposts. I furthered this by joining Nissan Buildings making crane jibs and cabs and became a qualified fitter welder.

1957 Desoto Firesweep – photo taken by kind permission of Alan Hills

1961 ...

First drag engine

In 1961 I got a job with Jack Oldings at Hatfield (this later became SLD Olding) as a service welder. I worked hard and long hours doing various welding assemblies for the construction industry. This was the year I purchased my very first engine for drag racing.

My first engine was a 3.4 MK7 Jaguar with a manual, 4 speed gearbox. I made a steel frame which could be built up and fitted with a small Marshall blower to the manifold. The blower was chain driven direct off the crank at the front,

without overdrive. The original one and three quarter SUs were modified and mounted on the blower. At that time my thoughts were, that I needed to enrich these SUs up about one hundred and fifty per cent. This I did, I made the jets and needles myself and fitted them.

I had the original starter with a battery standing on the floor. I held a gallon can of 'alky' about ten feet up on the crane, and believe it or not the darn thing started and ran continuously for about forty five seconds. I sort of stopped shaking and pulled the ignition wire off!

Over the next two years or so I was always reading the national motoring press having found the name of Sidney Allard who was attempting to build a V8 Chrysler engined dragster to promote the new sport of drag racing in England. I closely followed Allard's progress on his dragster as the following two years were also important to me when I put my engine into a car and my own car was born, the Houndog 1.

Sidney Allard's dragster

1962-63 ...

The birth of the Houndog 1

This was when my dreams and ambitions came to fruition. But it was also a year tinged with sadness as my dad died in 1962 of a heart attack. It was very sudden and happened when he was visiting his brother Bill in West Ham. So he never did get to see my success at drag racing, although I am sure he did watch over me from "above" as he always had great faith in me.

My friends Les Hill, George Myring, Ron Doyle, Colin Holloran and myself, in our spare time whilst still working at the Jack Olding's factory in Hatfield, helped build one of my first creations. It took us about eight months. It was mirrored on designs from America and based round a blown 3.4 litre Jaguar engine, Morris commercial rear axle, Mark 7 gearbox and Ford Popular front axle. It ran originally on Methanol with 10 – 12lb blower boost.

The story of "Nobby's Houndog 1" was covered in a write-up in the Herts Advertiser in October 1964, in Vickers News October 1964 and other magazines.

Why the name Houndog?

After completing the first dragster it became obvious I needed a really good name for it. I thought for a while, Garlits *(Swamp Rat),* Dean Moon *(Mooneyes),* Mickey Thompson *(Harvey Aluminum Special).* What did I like? Certainly I was a big fan of country music, and a new country singer in 1954-1955 the great Elvis, with his popular hit song "Houndog" was a favourite of mine. So this seemed just the right name for my newly built car from the first Houndog 1 right up to the new 2008 model, yes it worked well for me!

This is believed to be the first run a Houndog ever made!

1963 ... Awesome

Wow an American dragster at Silverstone

This is a year that I remember well, especially one day in September after reading a very tiny paragraph in the news about an American dragster that was going to be demonstrated at Silverstone the next day.

That was it, I immediately booked a days holiday and the next day I managed to arrive at Silverstone at 9.30am.

After driving up to the entrance I was not allowed in as it was a press day only. I was very disappointed, so I left the entrance and parked my car down the lane a little way. I sneaked in through a hole in the hedge and quickly walked to where the dragster was. It was then that I was approached by one of the gentlemen from the gate, he had obviously realised from my appearance that I was not really meant to be there. I did not want to lie so I took a chance and told the truth; I just really wanted to see the dragsters. Possibly my enthusiasm for the day just prevented him from calling a Marshall so I was allowed to stay. It was only later the following year when I met this man again that I realised this gentleman was Gerry Belton – thanks a lot.

What an awesome sight the Moon Eyes Dragster, Dean Moon, Dante Deuce and three other people were and being a country boy I sure loved what I saw! Cowboy boots, hats and white uniforms; the presentation was incredible and the Moon Eyes car, what can I say, the photos say it all! I was in Heaven! I was there when it happened so I guess

Americans at Silverstone:

Don Garlits, Dean Moon and Mickey Thompson

Nobby Hills

I ought to know.

Before my very eyes a blown Chevy, Potvin front mounted direct drive blower to a Halibrand quick change rear end, 7 inch firestone slicks and running on gas. At a later date I was able to buy these very slicks and run them on one of my cars!

Looking around it was just wonderful to see other British drag racers and their vehicles. Sidney Allard with his blown Hemi, Allan Allard with the Allardette, Alan Herridge and his blown straight 8 Buick, Tony Densham with the Worden Special, John Harrison with his dragster, George Brown with Super Nero, Bob and Roy Phelps, and probably more that I can remember.

NOBBY'S QUARTER MILE

As I walked back to the Moon Eyes team I stood very close so that I might hear what was being said. One comment that stood out came from Dante Deuce, he said, as I recall to Dean Moon, whilst looking at the slick, "so I don't think we're gonna break em loose", to which Dean replied, "I think we'd better give it a try". I was not at all sure at that time what they meant, after all it was 1963!

The next thing that happened was the Plymouth pick up of Fibre Glass Repairs came up behind the dragster and with Dante Deuce strapped in they proceeded to push the car up the strip, I did not know what to expect anyway, it did not fire up. It carried on to the end of the strip, turned round and proceeded to the start at increased speed, then all of a sudden the engine roared to life I had never heard a petrol engine sound so good, WOW!

TV Tommy Ivo

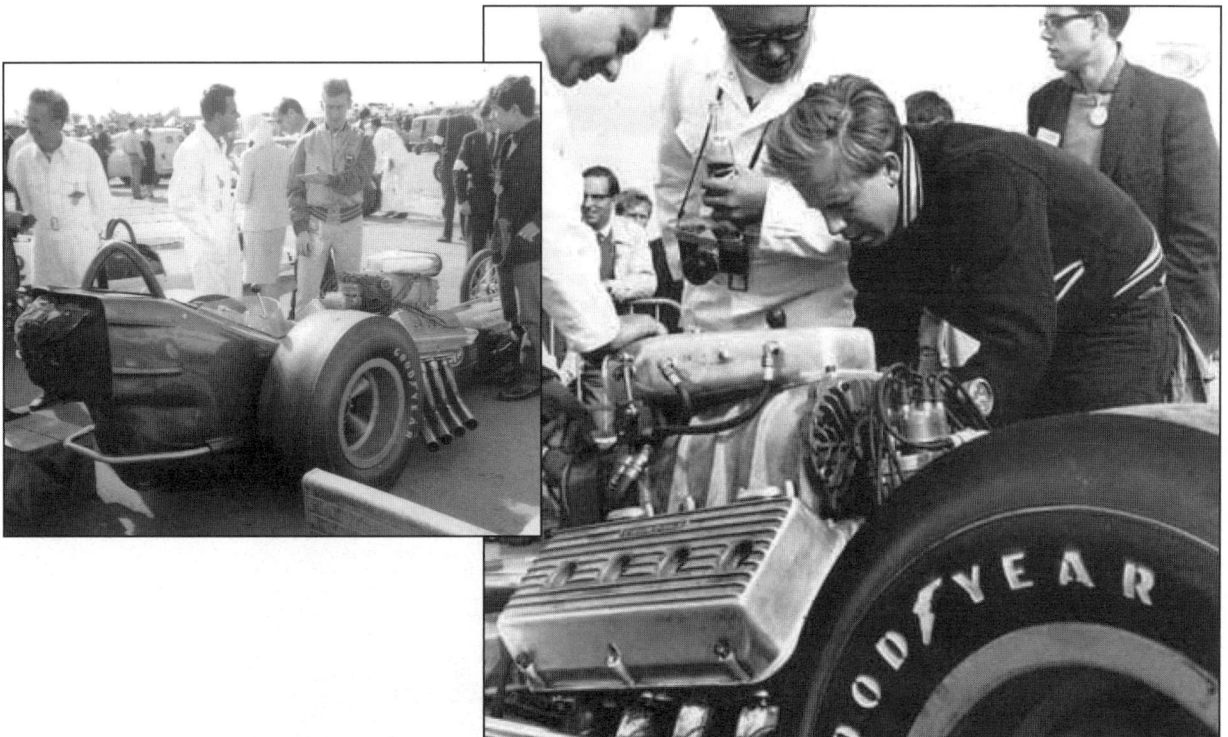

Gerry Belton:

Catch up time today with Mr. Gerry Belton here are his memories of his first meeting with Nobby

Gerry Belton, the man that Nobby claims changed his life in 1963, is now long retired, being even older than Nobby!

He was for some years PRO to Sydney Allard, one time famous car builder, hill climbing champion and South London main Ford dealer. Gerry recalls what led to his encounter with Nobby. It all began when, in 1961, Sydney decided we would build a

Mickey Thompson Harvey Aluminum Special.

big V8-powered dragster to help encourage drag racing in Britain.

The new car, with GMC-blown 5.8 litre Chrysler motor, was first shown to the media in July that year at Silverstone, where Sydney demonstrated the car over a timed quarter mile up the Club Straight. His best time was 9.5 seconds with an estimated terminal of 160mph. On one return run, he was alarmed to find two large pigs leisurely crossing his path, followed by two pigmen. One was heard later complaining of the possible effects 'on two valuable animals – one in pig as well!'

Reports of the new car were already creating interest in the States and, in 1963, as the result of a challenge made by the Moon Speed Equipment Company of Santa Fe, a team arrived in England to take on Allard with their Chevrolet-engined dragster, Mooneyes, to be driven by one Dante Deuce. We had already formed the British Drag Racing Association (BDRA) and began planning a big drag racing event for 1964, the British International Drag Festival, to which would be invited a number of top US cars and bikes.

With drag racing still virtually unknown in the UK, we decided that the Deuce/Allard challenge could be built up so as to provide valuable publicity for the Festival which was already promising to be a hugely complex and costly undertaking. So we booked Silverstone again, this time for a Press Day on Tuesday 10th September.

To add further spice to the Deuce/Allard challenge races, we had invited two representatives of the newly emerging British drag racing scene, Tony Densham with his Ford powered 'Worden', and the Buick-engined dragster of Alan Herridge.

Nobby Hills

George Brown's blown Vincent 'Super Nero' would also effectively represent the motorcycle quarter mile brigade. The day was strictly for the press and television people only. This was not only to help me control the event, as I would know every single person present, but also to meet insurance conditions and RAC regulations. Which meant no public whatsoever.

The day was going splendidly. But then, I caught sight of an unfamiliar figure, hovering in the background and obviously hoping not to be noticed. I finally came up to him, a not too scruffy chap in his late twenties, and would have asked him to produce his pass. Enough to say, it was obvious that he shouldn't be there. But instead of trying to bull**** his way out of his situation, he simply said he'd heard about the day and so badly wanted to be there that he'd taken the risk of being caught. Which he definitely had been! I should have got a marshall to see him out. But so impressed was I by his honesty and enthusiasm that I told him he could stay but to keep well out of the way. I probably also said that he should tell anyone that challenged him that he was there on my authority.

Come to think of it, I'm sure I never even asked his name. But I was very soon to become aware of it, as Nobby, to his great credit, was to be one of the British dragster entries in the following year's Drag Festival. And we all know the rest!

A special weekend in 1963

The following weekend I was informed that Mickey Thompson had arrived in the UK with his Harvey Aluminum Special (I think this is the car that eventually became Commuter). I also found out that he was going to Madeira Drive, Brighton and the next weekend at Debden. I was unable to make Brighton where Mickey set the straw bales alight with the flames from his headers. But I made Debden and as per usual I tried to get as close as possible to him and Dean Moon.

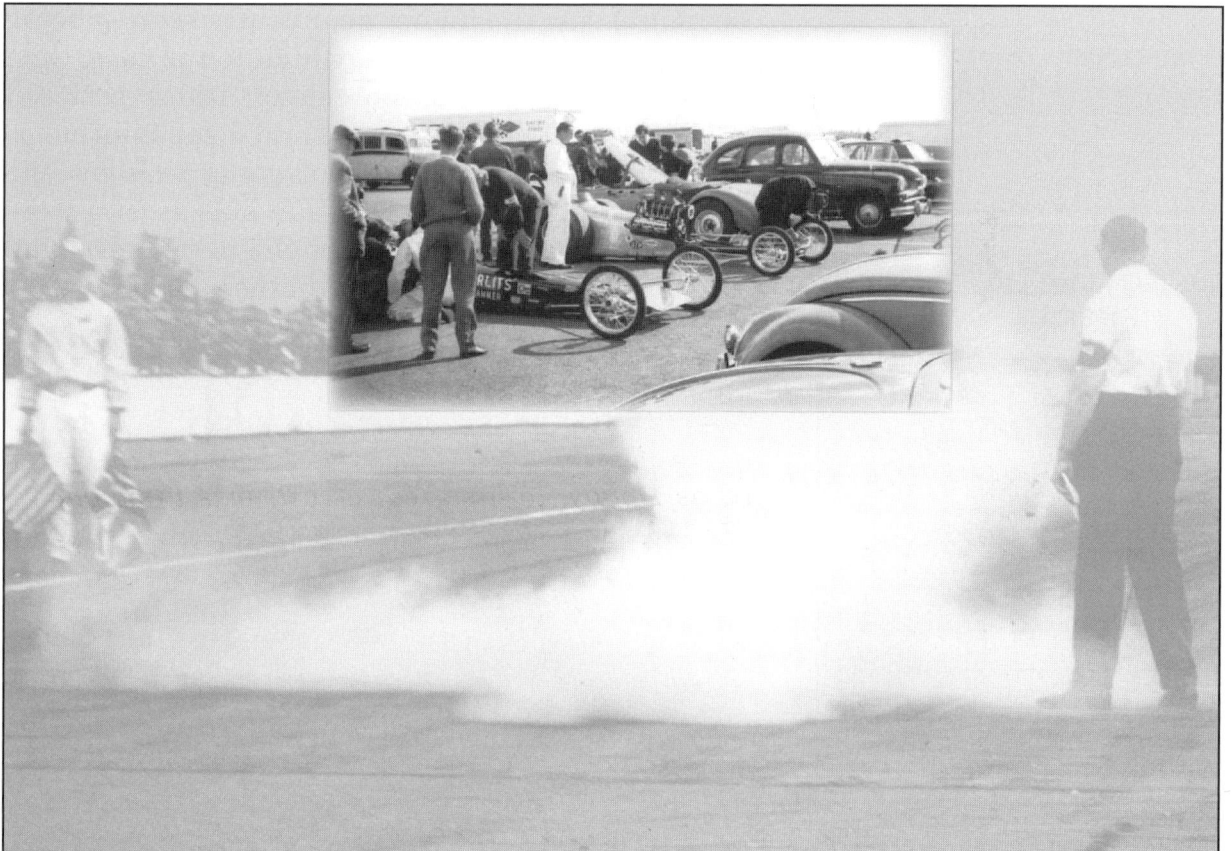

The standing start quarter and half mile were set up side by side. I think Mickey's speed was up to about 170mph in the quarter but also in attendance was George Brown with Super Nero. I am fairly sure George was recording about 200 mph in the half mile which was the highest speed recorded during the weekend. I was close enough to M.T. to hear him say to his hepper, "do we have the high gear rear end with us?" To which his hepper said, "yes". Mickey immediately said, "get that centre section out we will run over 200 mph in the half mile this afternoon". I was starting to get excited now – any car doing 200 mph in 1963 has got to be seen!

Off came the wheels, and out came the centre section. I saw the higher gear centre section being unwrapped and made ready to fit to the case; then there was some anxious conversations between MT crew and the RAC people and disappointment. It seemed the RAC were not going to allow the dragster to try and run 200 mph plus as they were not "geared up for it". I thought to myself, "well this is England but I'd had another super day!"

The first British drag festival 1964 ...

The Houndog 1 competed at the First British Drag Festival in 1964. The first meeting was held at Blackbushe Airport on 19th September and the Houndog 1 was designated dragster number 72 and ran the following times:

19.47 secs at 64 m.p.h. terminal 1st run
17.67 secs at 77 m.p.h. terminal 2nd run
16.27 secs at 84 m.p.h. terminal 3rd run

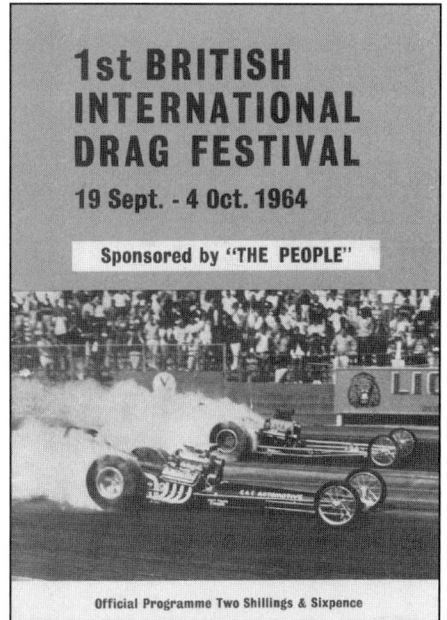

1st BRITISH INTERNATIONAL DRAG FESTIVAL
19 Sept. - 4 Oct. 1964
Sponsored by "THE PEOPLE"
Official Programme Two Shillings & Sixpence

At this particular meeting the famous Don Garlits ran 8.28 secs, Tommy Ivo 8.46 secs, Tony Nancy 9.41 secs and one British entrant Alan Allard in the Allard Dragon ran 11.42 secs.

Further on in the sixth of the series of meetings, which was also held at Blackbushe Airport on the 4th October 1964 I was able to better the time in the Houndog by two seconds with Les Hill driving the dragster as at previous meetings – dragster number 120 ran 14.46 seconds. Again the time for the Americans was somewhat faster with Don Garlits running 8.12 secs, Tommy Ivo running 8.21 secs and Tony Nancy running 9.57 secs. Alan Allard again had a slower time of 10.28 secs in the Allard Dragster and diminutive Alan Herridge running a Buick 8 ran a 14.36 secs.

After the first Drag Festival I dismantled the old car and designed a new one still using the 3.4 MK 7 Jaguar engine. There were so many improvements I needed to incorporate. New rear and front end motor cycle wheels, pressurised fuel tanks, bigger blower, more fuel.

1964 ...

Woburn Abbey

Woburn Abbey, the home of the Duke and Duchess of Bedford, was one of the many venues I visited to show the Houndog 2. We often got many people looking at the cars at these events. I remember once when I was standing at the rear of the car and a very young lad came and looked at the car. He was with his father and as he got to the chute pack he said to his dad, "look dad that's where you put the sandwiches!" Alan Herridge also came along to this show he always had a big smile on his face when he tried to explain the construction of the cars to visitors. There were also pop groups performing in the grounds and with the UK's first hot rods and dragsters on show this was a good way of getting people interested in the cars and introducing drag racing into this country.

A new parachute

I needed a new chute for this second car. There was only one way as I couldn't afford a new one, so I decided I would make one. I made a 14ft cross form in blue nylon. I worked it out from photographs of American parachutes that I had seen. I nearly wore out my mother's Singer sewing machine, there were five three sixteenth nylon lines on each of the sections these were all stitched 100 per cent. They were 20ft from the fixing on the car to the start of the cross. This made 540ft of nylon with 280ft of stitching on the cords alone. I got there eventually. Now for the testing.

It had to work when fitted to the dragster. I went out looking for a country road which I found about two miles from my home. I then drove up and down a few times to check it out, there was not a lot of traffic on the roads back in 1964. Right I'm ready, I wrapped the new spliced lines around my right hand wrist and drove along at about 15mph, great. I then threw the chute out, the wind was fine, the chute hit the road surface and just simply dragged along the road surface behind the car. I can only say I was very disappointed. What now? I gathered up the chute and folded it down again. I went back down the road and sat awhile thinking.

It was so obvious! I just did my first test at 15mph and the dragster would be doing over 100mph. I just had to do the same thing, but go a lot faster. This time I wrapped the lines around my wrist again I then drove along the road at about 40mph, I threw up the chute out of the window I don't think it touched the road this time. Well what happened next I had the lines wrapped around my wrist about half a dozen times and I could not let go of them. I really felt like my right arm and shoulder were going to leave my body by the time I had applied the foot brake. After the pain had gone away I sat for about fifteen minutes or so. I then laughed, gathered up the chute and drove home very pleased with the chute working.

When it was eventually fixed on the dragster it worked fantastically being used up to 140mph or more so it was well worth it in the end but I still think my right arm is a little longer than my left!

Back end view of Houndog

1965 ...

The debut of the Houndog 2

In June of this year the British Hot Rod Association had their first competition meeting of the year, in conjunction with the British Drag Racing Association, at the Royal Air Force Station at Duxford.

It was during the next five years that I was also given fantastic help from Bob and Roy Phelps, Peter Billinton and the co-directors of Jack Oldings which helped us get going enormously.

We built this Houndog still using a 3.4 MK 7 Jaguar engine which we picked up from the Exchange and Mart magazine for a mere £15. The motor was stock as were the heads.

A Wade blower was fitted which was front mounted, driven with four V belts from the front of the crankshaft. The inlet manifolding was short and functional and the carburettion was by three one and three quarter inch SU carburettors with the blower being overdriven by 27% so that the pressure was between sixteen and eighteen pounds per square inch.

The top three gears of the Jaguar gearbox were used and the drive passed through a

Rare photo of Nobby actually driving a dragster!

3.1:1 drive. It had a Chrysler rear axle narrowed to thirty six inch and the brakes and rear wheels were also Chrysler, the former being hydraulic and operated by a hand lever.

The chassis front frame I designed and constructed from a one and three quarter inch, sixteen gauge cold drawn steel tube with one inch by sixteen gauge being used for the front half of the lower frame tube and diagonals. A substantial roll bar with a good clearance between the top of the driver's helmet and the crest of the cage was made from one and three quarter inch by five thirty seconds of an inch wall thickness.

On the whole gas welding was used but there was

PRACTICE DAY PANORAMA

Picture shows some of the dragsters which appeared at a recent Graveley Practice Day. From left to right they are: Norman Hills' Houndog II; Dragster Developments' Cadillac Dragster; The Road Runner; Dave Metcalfe with his TR2 Dragster; The Square One Dragster of Leon Moss; Les Turner's beautifully engineered Ford Dragster; Denis Jenkinson's Bristol-Dragon; Harold Bull and his sweet A30 Mini-dragster. B.D.R. magazine now has a list of 23 dragsters currently being built and the success of future practice days seems well assured.

a little electric arc welding. Originally the front axle was one and a half inches, sixteen gauge but as there were signs that it was bending, I decided it should be changed to one and five eighth inches, twelve gauge in stainless steel.

The front tyres were Avon on Honda rims, home made hubs were fitted to Anglia spindles and a home made torsion bar and shockers were fitted. The chassis weight was one hundred and thirteen pounds with fuel, giving an overall weight of eleven hundredweight.

The whole frame was used as a pressure reservoir for the fuel tank. Steering was through a Ford Mark 1 box and the body panels were made of sixteen gauge half hard aluminium. The rear tyres were Goodyear Blue Streak 7.50 x 15 and were run at a pressure of forty five pounds per square inch.

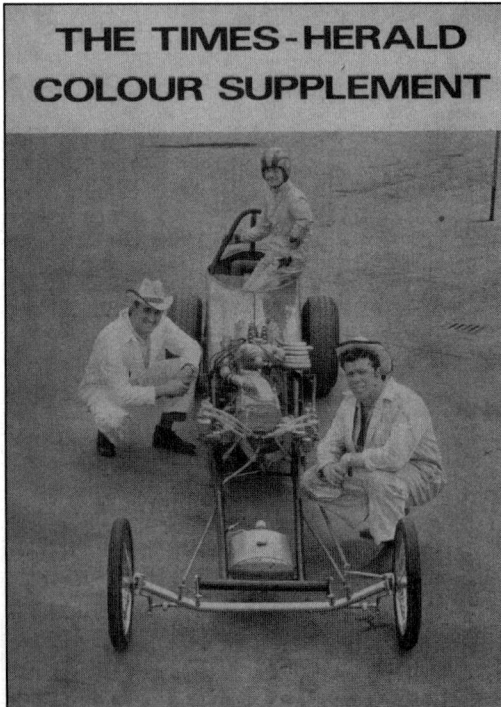

THE TIMES-HERALD
COLOUR SUPPLEMENT

June 6th 1965 ...

My first trophy ... success!

On Whit Sunday, June 6th my car won my first trophies and I was very proud of myself and my excellent team Les Hill and Ron Doyle and at last felt my drag racing was going somewhere good.

I won the "Percentage Improved Performance Trophy" presented to me by the British Drag Racing Magazine and also the "Best Performance

British Hot Rod Association Member Trophy.

I was even mentioned in the British Drag Racing magazine, which was the official journal of the British Drag Racing Association.

Quote by Roland Green the Editor at the time:

"I shall publish few pictures during 1965 which give me as much pleasure as the one showing Norman Hills (that's Nobby) receiving the British Drag Racing Magazine Trophy for the most improved performance won with Houndog 2. As one who has had the pleasure of receiving letters from Norman telling of the trials and tribulations and the doubts and fears harboured for Houndog 2, I must say that I feel his success at the British Hot Rod Association Whitsun Meet was as much deserved as it was obviously popular.

During his success Norman Hills did not forget the rest of his team, Les Hill and Ron Doyle. Still clasping his trophy his first request, was, 'where can I buy two more trophies to give to my team'. British Drag Racing Magazine presents these additional trophies with compliments and considers it a privilege to do so.

Houndog 2 had many problems to overcome, not the least being the lack of cash. Here the good friends of this budding sport Valvoline oiled the wheels a little. Norman, Les and Ron are not to be congratulated just because they won a trophy, they deserve our congratulations because they met a challenge, had faith in their machine and themselves. They are typical of many others, who, in workshops up and down the country, are devoting their time, their money and their skills to the new sport of drag racing – we welcome them."

1965 ...
The second British Drag Festival

I was proud to present the Houndog 2 at this event held at Blackbushe Airport on 25th and 26th September. This meeting was organised by the British Drag Racing Association.

In an article in the programme I noticed it explained to people how cheap it was to build a dragster, Houndog 2 being classed as a £250 dragster and Houndog 1 as a £100 dragster.

At this event the Houndog 2 was credited as being the longest wheel base of the British cars that competed in Class 4 team dragsters of 2.5 to 5 litre capacity. The car number was 214 and the driver was Les Hill. A typical result from this dragster was 11.7 at 130mph.

Unfortunately this event suffered from typical doses of the great British rain, nothing ever changes, and although the visitors from the USA did wet runs for demonstration purposes, the dragster times (British and American) were not at their best.

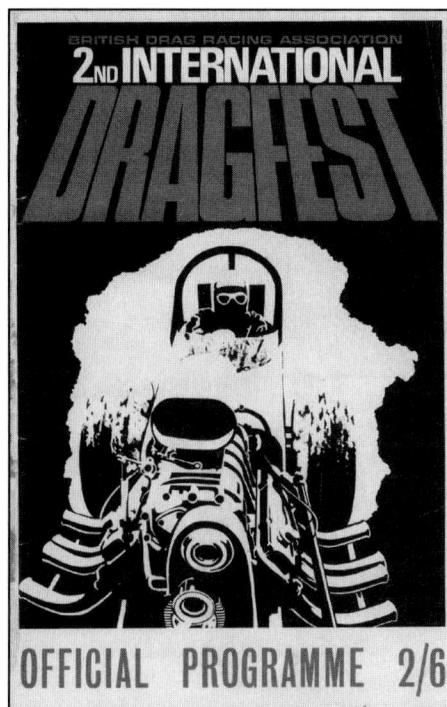

BRITISH DRAG RACING ASSOCIATION
2ND INTERNATIONAL DRAGFEST
OFFICIAL PROGRAMME 2/6

Mechanic
2nd INTERNATIONAL
DRAGFEST 1965
MOTOR RACING IS DANGEROUS
Your attention is drawn to the warning printed on the reverse

Zandvort 1968 Alf Hagon

Alf Hagon ... top all-rounder

One of the greatest all-rounders, Alf Hagon was a grass-track champion, professional speedway rider, top drag racer and world-speed record holder. Hagon, whose innocuous looks belied his competitive nature, first went grass racing in his native Essex during the 1940s. Success attracted sponsors and Hagon became one of Britain's top grass trackers, winning 11 national championships. Between 1953 and 1965, he rode for several of the country's First Division speedway teams.

Inspirations on direct drive

When I met Alf at Graveley in 1964 (for practice drag racing) and then again in 1965 we spoke as he was in the process of trying to run a sub-ten second pass. After much thought Alf's idea to improve his performance was to be a direct

drive set up on his motorbike (a V twin engine Jap as I recall). I found this idea extremely interesting and after a few more conversations with Alf and my admiration for his engineering ability made me think towards a direct drive set up for the next car (Houndog 3). Although I knew at the present time the Jaguar powered rail was not producing enough power to run this set up, more conversations with Alf and I was truly inspired to give direct drive a go and, with the extra Cadillac power on the Houndog 3 this is just what we did. Thank you Alf for your many conversations which did give me the right ideas and help.

I also met his wife Jean and was introduced to his new baby daughter Julie and we all enjoyed many a conversation on engines, bikes and cars!

On catching up with Alf in later years I was pleased to recall he remembered these days and also our conversations on direct drive on his motorbike and the effects it had on the dragsters.

Alf and Jean commented:

"We were very pleased when Nobby contacted Alf in September 2007. Forty three years is a very long time and meeting again was just so amazing and once we started talking the fond memories of those times at Graveley and the first Drag Fest all came flooding back to us. Today we feel a great admiration for Nobby as much as he in those early years showed Alf, and are inspired by the fact after seeing his drawings of his future project in drag racing he will continue to be a great success. The fact that Alf inspired him to give direct drive a go on his Houndog car is a very great tribute indeed."

Nobby and Alf Hagon meet up in 2007 again

1966 ... Santa Pod
The Phelps family

This was the year that the old airfield was converted into a permanent drag strip. It was to be called Santa Pod. The name originated from the famous Santa Ana drag strip in the USA and the combination of the local village name being Podington.

The Phelps Family – Bob and his son Roy, along with Santa Pod's administrator Eileen Cattley - had a huge impact on British drag racing. They were involved from its very early days of the Drag Fests but really only became main players with the opening of Santa Pod Raceway in 1966 which they continued to run into the 1990s. They were personally involved in building many of the facilities at the track including the tower, barriers, and the famous Barn. Bob and Roy also ran their own stable of race cars. Roy drove the Gloworm Capri Funny Car and the Wheelie Stingray, which is still running today. The Phelps family not only ran their own cars, but helped many other teams with parts, as well as building their engines for them.

Stingray Wheelie Car driven by Roy Phelps

NOBBY'S QUARTER MILE

A string of big name USA drivers came to Britain to race at Santa Pod Raceway. All these cars and teams were bought over by the Phelps family, usually with the cars staying to be raced by British drag racers afterwards. The list of these famous names included Paula Murphy, Don Garlits, Gene Snow, Raymond Beadle, Don Schumacher, Sammy Miller, Tony Nancy, Al Segrini and Darrell Gywnn. They signed an agreement with the International Drag Racing Association from the USA to run Santa Pod under the IHRA banner. Santa Pod became the only facility in Europe to be an official IHRA sanctioned track.

1990 was significant for the Phelps family and also for British drag racing as the owner of the land decided to sell. After the sale of the land Roy decided to sell the separate company name of Santa Pod Raceway to the same people buying the land. The Phelps family had a great impact on the sport and its growth over the many years that they were the owners of Santa Pod Raceway. Sadly Bob Phelps died in 1988. Roy Phelps carried on running Santa Pod until 1990.

Commuter driven by Tony Densham

Roy Phelps and Gloworm

Bob Phelps

Nobby remembers

Bob & Roy Phelps

I think the first time I saw Bob and Roy was in 1963 at Silverstone although we did not actually speak until after the first Drag Fest, when I had built the Houndog 2 and I took it to Santa Pod Raceway early in 1965 to do the first test runs.

I warmed the engine and prepared for a run up the strip, this was when the start line was about where the finish line is now, no tower, white fencing and a man with a big brush painting the fence. There were no other people visible at the time. I said to the driver Les Hill, "I don't know if we will be able to run or not with the fence being painted at the start line": Anyway we push started the car and Les approached the start line. Just as he was getting to the line, the gent with paintbrush ran to the centre of the strip in front of the dragster. I thought here's the first problem and to my amazement he beckoned Les forward to the start line and used his large paint brush to give the dragster a flag start. There then began

Commuter

a fantastic relationship (yes the man with the paintbrush was Bob Phelps the owner) with Bob Phelps and the Phelps family including Eileen for the next twenty five years.

I don't know whether I was just lucky or whether they saw something in my enthusiasm and car building capability but over the next twenty years or more they supported me fantastically, providing me with the best parts that were available over these years such as a complete ready built Ed Pink FC engine, all I had to do was bolt it in and apply the starter. They also provided brand new Crower Glide clutches, brand new reversers, a brand new Lenco FC rear axle. These were wonderful times and both my cars performed very well with the times and the speeds speaking for themselves.

I will always be thankful for the support of Bob and Roy Phelps for the Houndog team which made for very happy times!

Firefly

Nobby ...

by Roy Phelps

My first recollection of drag racing dates back to 1963, when my cousin John Bennett and I visited Silverstone for this country's historic first exposure to the might and power of American top fuel dragsters. Such an auspicious occasion naturally attracted the cream of British drag racing, of which two entrants of the day were to later play a part in my life – Alan Herridge and Nobby Hills.

Nobby Hills is best remembered as the driving force behind the famous series of top fuelers and funny cars bearing the Houndog name. Nobby was in his first season as an owner/builder, campaigning a very British Jaguar powered dragster. Although modest by today's standards this car carried the name Houndog and therefore can be credited with pioneering the Houndog phenomenon.

Though impressed with the sight and sound of drag

racing at Silverstone, I went back to South London to continue working at Fibre Glass Repairs. In my absence Nobby continued to pursue his interest in drag racing, running the supercharged Jaguar whenever possible.

By 1965 my dad Bob Phelps, had become involved with a project to build a dragstrip on the old Podington airfield. A considerable amount of work was required to provide even the most basic of infrastructure in order to turn the dream into a reality. Many enthusiasts donated their time and experience in creating Europe's first dragstrip. One of those was Nobby Hills whose work provided a number of items that we now all take for granted such as the barriers and the water tanks required for the toilets. It was during this period that a bond between Nobby and my family grew into a lifetime friendship. Nobby's racing experience was expanding and by the time Santa Pod Raceway opened under the name of National Dragways in 1966 his cars had already gained a reputation as being immaculately turned out and pretty reliable.

Aerial view of Santa Pod way back in 1943!

As time progressed, the Houndog car evolved into the Houndog team with Mike Hutcherson becoming the regular driver as performance increased and crowd support for the team became more visible. When Mike Hutcherson suffered a tyre failure and a subsequent collision with the barrier, Fibre Glass Repairs had no hesitation in helping and supplying the tubing for a new Houndog chassis.

Though Houndog was popular at Santa Pod and was attracting a hard core of supporters the Cadillac engined dragsters were lacking the power of the FGR hemi Chryslers. With the team being so popular and Nobby still spending time

working to improve the infrastructure of Santa Pod, the bond between Nobby and Bob Phelps, Santa Pod's director was key to bringing Houndog 5 into life. Nobby building the chassis and Bob supplying Houndog's first blown hemi by way of a new 354 Chrysler. This put Houndog into the 8's and significantly increased the number of Houndog followers. We were delighted as it helped to increase Santa Pod's loyal band of spectators. A year or so later Nobby acquired his first 392 hemi from Firefly and Houndog instantly dropped into the sevens.

Life was changed for all of us in 1973, when Fibre Glass Repairs purchased the two American funny cars brought over to this country by Don Schumacher and Paula Murphy. Alan Herridge was the obvious choice to drive Don Schumacher's Stardust and Bob and I felt that there was only one person to look after and maintain the ex Paula Murphy STP car. When Bob told Nobby that he could take it home, he seemed to be in a state of shock. He joked later that he 'slept with the car for a week' in order to take it all in.

Nobby soon showed that he was the right man to look after and maintain this car, the result of which it is still remembered today as one of the most popular cars ever to run in this country. From that dreamy drive home there was no holding back the legend that became the Houndog Racing Team.

Nobby and I retired from drag racing but remained firm life long friends, so when he told me that he intended to build one last Houndog funny car, I felt it only right to support him and to help to get that engine lit up and those tyres smoking again.

Roy Phelps.

1965-1966 ...

Houndog 3

During late 1965 I met Mr Movin' Mike Hutcherson. He worked with me and I was soon excited when I learnt that he worked on test driving for Lotus. So it seemed he was a very natural choice and was offered the hot seat for the newly built Houndog 3.

The next three years were a little difficult as I found it difficult to get the engines to rev properly. They were fine standing and idling so I made all my own fuel injection systems and made up the inlet manifold, which had a much larger flow. Also the blower drive was my own design. The reasoning was if I need something I could not afford I made it. So it was a good job I had become very mechanically minded and with my welding skills this bode me well.

This was chrome yellow and mid blue Cadillac block and rear axle, the front axle was from the Houndog 2. The car had a full body in the style of Gentleman Joe Shuebeck's 65 Schneider Cam Special, the tail end was similar to Tony Nancy's '22' Junior.

Pics show top to bottom: Mike Hutcherson in the cockpit

Outside The Bargeman Pub

Nobby receives the first trophy

Model shoot at Santa Pod

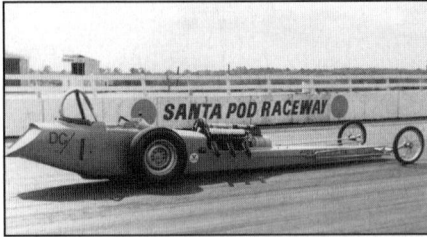

The progress of the Houndog 3 was reported in many magazines:

Drag Racing and Hot Rod Association in May 1966: *"Houndog 3 is nearly completed, it has a 154 in wheelbase and American style body and 1955 Cadillac 5.7 litre engine bored 40 thou, 7:1 pistons 323 cu.in. Wade blower, custom built double disc clutch and direct drive unit".*

September 1966 saw the first outing of the Houndog 3 here Movin' Mike Hutcherson struggled to push the Houndog 3 across the finish line after a 7.24 run, that is 7 minutes 24 seconds!

By October 1966 according to the Drag Racing and Hot Rod: "Alan Herridge is eliminated by Movin' Mike".

Towards the end of this year I decided to rest the car and remove the Wade blower and fit 4 SU carburettors mounted on ram stacks as a temporary measure as the injector blower did have a few problems.

By the next year I was surprised to see my Houndog 3 on the front cover of the Drag Racing and Hot Rod magazine.

1966 ... Meeting the famous

Anthony Armstrong Jones later to become Lord Snowdon

I met Anthony Armstrong Jones in 1966 when he was on a photo shoot for the Hanson Trust, a parent company of SLDO in Hatfield. He was a very professional photographer and I was so impressed with the photographs that he took of the people who worked there at the time. The photograph he took of myself was extremely flattering. He later married Princess Margaret The Queen's sister and was known as Lord Snowdon, a very pleasant and professional man indeed.

Graham and Betty Hill and Damon Hill the future Formula One racing driver

I organised the Ware Motor Club Show at the Ware Drill Hall and Graham Hill was invited to open the event. He brought along his wife Betty and their son Damon who at the time must have been about five. Little was I to guess that this young chap was to follow in his father's footsteps in the Formula One racing car stakes.

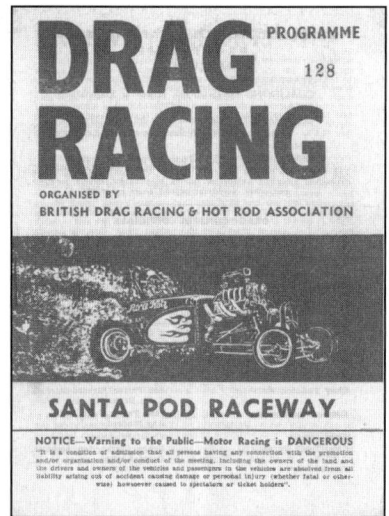

DRAG RACING

PROGRAMME 128

ORGANISED BY
BRITISH DRAG RACING & HOT ROD ASSOCIATION

SANTA POD RACEWAY

NOTICE—Warning to the Public—Motor Racing is DANGEROUS

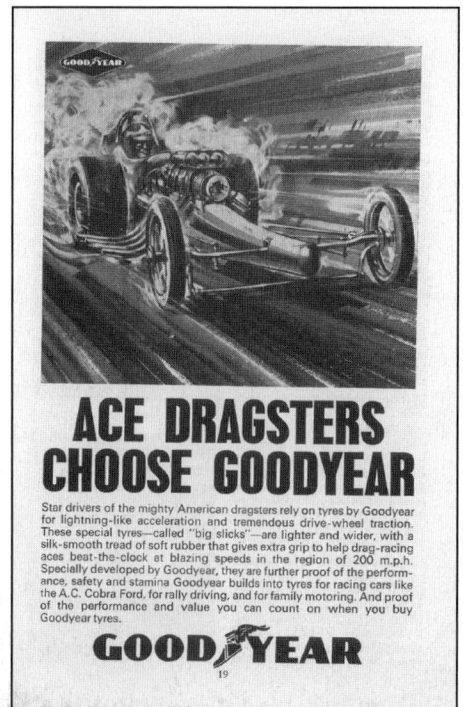

ACE DRAGSTERS CHOOSE GOODYEAR

Star drivers of the mighty American dragsters rely on tyres by Goodyear for lightning-like acceleration and tremendous drive-wheel traction. These special tyres—called "big slicks"—are lighter and wider, with a silk-smooth tread of soft rubber that gives extra grip to help drag-racing aces beat-the-clock at blazing speeds in the region of 200 m.p.h. Specially developed by Goodyear, they are further proof of the performance, safety and stamina Goodyear builds into tyres for racing cars like the A.C. Cobra Ford, for rally driving, and for family motoring. And proof of the performance and value you can count on when you buy Goodyear tyres.

GOOD/YEAR

1966 to 1967 ...

Perfecting the Houndog 4

It was at this time I decided the only way to go was a V8 as there was no substitute for cubic inches. I finished up finding a source for 372 cubic inch Cadillacs which were being used for stock car racing in the UK. So I designed and built this car using stainless steel for the chassis and all the steering and suspension tubes using longer torsion arms on the front.

NOBBY'S QUARTER MILE

Modifications to 372 caddy blocks: these engines did not have an oil filter so I was able to make an exit to a filter unit and a return to the block. Also the three centre main bearing housings were machined and a girdle made which was then fitted to keep everything in place. This necessitated manufacturing a new oil pan. The other thing which I did to the block was to overbore it into the water jacket. I then fitted larger bore engine sleeves and then bored these out to fit the pistons. Also the block and the heads were o-ring grooved and stainless steel wires were fitted. Another job was grinding the oil-grooves on the crank to double the size to allow a better flow of oil. Then the pistons were fitted with tougher quality pins and teflon buttons. After breaking five engines in one year I found this was well worth the times we achieved.

Nobby Hills

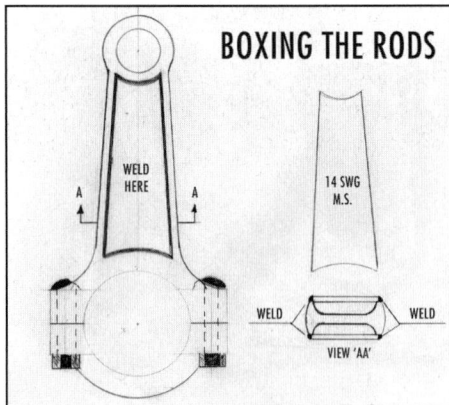

Nobby's drawing of his rod strengthening techniques

I had to increase the diameter of the crankshaft nose by ¼inch to stop the blower drive from bending it. This I did by cutting off the original and welding on a larger diameter nose.

During this time I was working my way up to a staff job and became a charge-hand in the welding and assembly workshop. I must have been trying hard because I was allowed to use a spare lock up unit besides the transport workshop which was ideal for my racing and helped immensely with my now fast growing hobby.

It did involve many long hours with a heavy work load. I was able to start on the car at 5am until 8am and then work 8am until 6.30pm for the company and then do another two hours on the car, seven days a week so it really was an all time consuming project.

Engine problems then were as common as they can be today but then we did not have any electronic testing machines or such like. It was a case of keeping very much to "back to basics" so when the American Commando Drag Racing Team came to SPR I examined their set up pretty closely and was able to evaluate a really basic problem with my set up. Fuel flow!

I had an offset gear diesel pump from a cement mixer (as per usual compromising again) which I had modified to pump this alky mix but I only had a ¾inch bore feed to it. I increased this to 1¼inch bore and never looked back. The car immediately revved to where it wanted to be.

Another thing I remember that I did on these Caddies was to modify the hydraulic lifters to being solid. This amounted to removing the centre from the hydraulic cam followers and replacing it

BOXING THE RODS

with a solid piece machined by Mike Hutcherson. I then cut the end off the rocker arms and replace them with a welded on threaded end that would accept Ford adjusters and Ford push rods. The machine work again was carried out by Mike Hutcherson. The cams were reground by Piper Cams and they were very successful. Another major job was boxing the rods I used to hand cut 14 SWG MS. This was to fit on the sides of the rods and weld them in, they were then straightened and the bearing ends checked for round. This all worked a treat, i.e. 10.52 ET – 150 mph!

Peter Billinton also gave me excellent advice for which I am forever thankful. Thanks a bunch Peter.

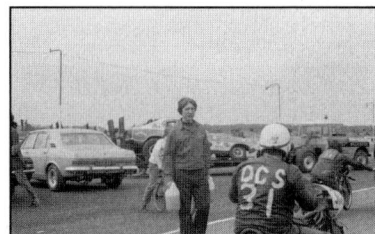

Peter Billinton in the pits at Santa Pod

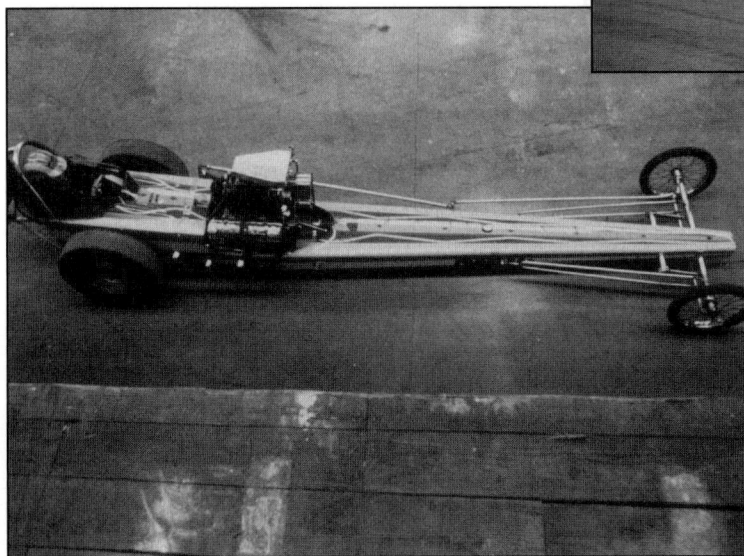

"BIG GO"
May 25th

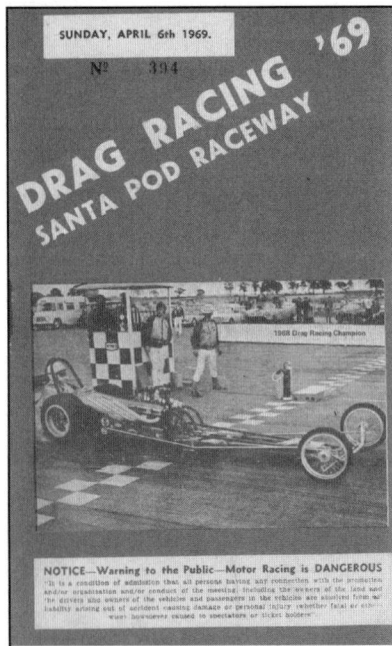

1968 ...

We were classed as the "in thing" by one article:

Nobby Hills and driver Movin' Mike Hutcherson and "Houndog" along with several interesting changes including the 1968 "in thing" for drag racing automobiles – horizontal stripes, being of course in the team colours of blue and yellow, for this well known Cadillac powered car. During the winter the blower has received great attention. Firstly it is now driven via rubber doughnut coupling instead of a duplex chain from the front of the engine. The supercharger has been turned completely over so that the orifice originally used for the forward facing single large bore injector now serves as the outlet to the new plumbing to the inlet ports. Consequently, what was the outlet is now the inlet for twin semi-down-draught injectors made by the team. Protruding saucily through the bodywork is a gleaming chrome fuel tank with conical rear end for efficient fuel flow. Finally, a new steel clutch has been fabricated. All this seems to work for our friends.

Mike returning to the pits

1970 ...

March 23 – A Sunday motorist parachutes into Piccadilly

I was called by an Italian advertising company and asked if I would do a demonstration in the Piccadilly Underpass. I could not believe my ears. "Yes Sir", I replied, on which the gentleman said, "Sunday morning 7.00am 22nd March, giving me three weeks notice.

Also invited to take part in this was Bill Weichelt and his car Dos Palmos known as "Wild Bill". He

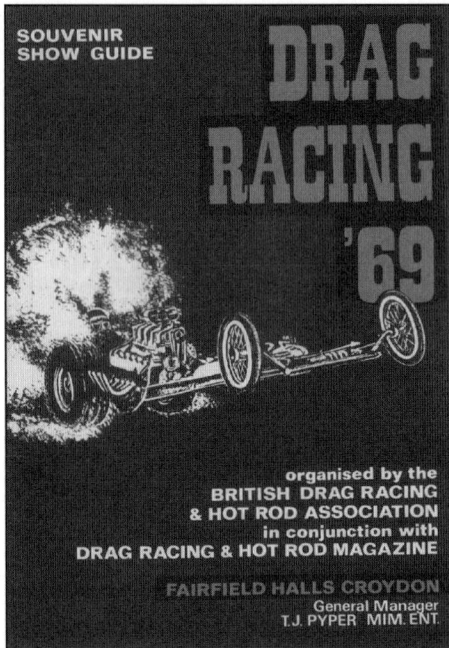

The Daily Mirror giving us a mention

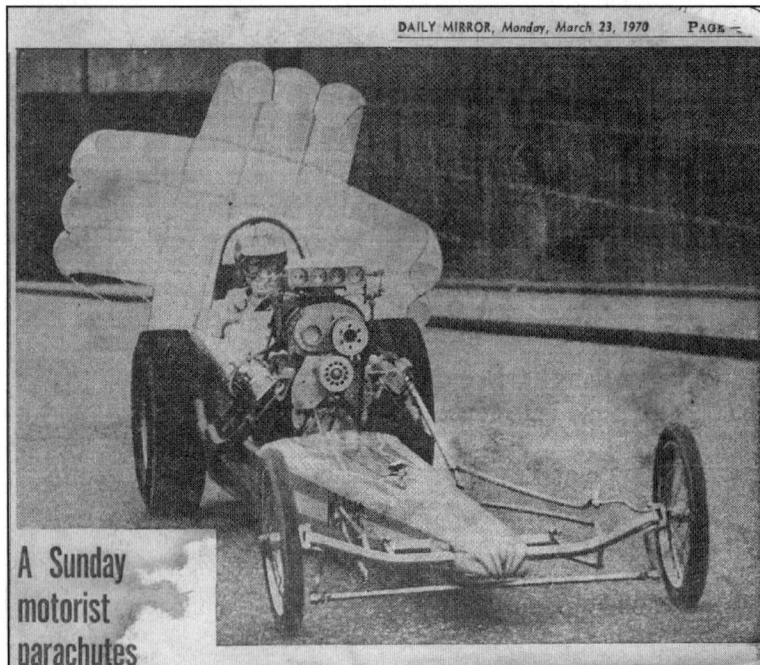

had been in the UK since 1967. (See below news clipping about him).

The day arrived and we all assembled at Piccadilly Circus as well as all the TV crews. Obviously there were a lot of police who would close off the underpass. As it happened we had to go the opposite way to the traffic and I was assured by the police that there would be no problem and they stopped the traffic entering the underpass.

I was told when ready, off you go with the truck and trailer. I moved off towards Kensington and then I had to mount the pavement to enable me to get the rig into the underpass going the wrong way without unhitching the trailer. (This being a Dually and 40ft tag long trailer so very long indeed!)

That was fine but when I made the return into the tunnel a cabbie decided that I was making a wrong turn. I explained to him that the Police had stopped the traffic from entering the other end but he would have none of it. Anyway I had to get out of the truck and tell him to go away!

I then went round into the underpass unloaded the dragster and prepared for a run. Once both cars were ready I took over the situation. I instructed Bill and Mike after a push-start to proceed to the lowest point where I would be standing in an adjoining passage with flag, where I gave both dragsters a flag start. It was fantastic, the noise was unbelievable, both dragsters left the underpass, the police did not know what was going on and both cars stopped nearby in the traffic safely and were featured in the daily papers.

Quoted from a newspaper cutting:

Don't look now but someone's doing a cool 80mph right in the middle of London. Admittedly Mike Hutcherson has got better brakes than the average weekend motorist. He released a parachute to slow him down as he hurtled out of the underpass into Piccadilly yesterday in his dragster car, Houndog. Dragsters – cars designed solely for the thrill of tremendous acceleration have long been a craze in America. But it's doubtful if they will ever become very common in Piccadilly.

Mike of Welwyn Garden City, Herts let Houndog off the leash for an advertising film.

"WILD BILL" ...

Bill Weichelt had arrived in the UK in 1967, posted by Uncle Sam to serve in the US Air Force. After some time crewing for Dennis Priddle and Rex Sluggett on Tudor Rose and racing his own Mini Cooper in Junior Street he obtained the Dos Palmos car from Keith Schellenberg in 1969. Having already had experience of driving many vehicles, including fuelers, in the States, he soon mastered the now unfashionable short wheel based car and before long became known as 'Wild Bill'.

Bill Weichelt – Wild Bill

Nobby Hills

1970 saw Bill trash the motor before getting the car back into the low eights with a best of 8.3/182, it was running as well as it ever had in the States half a decade earlier. At Santa Pods August Championships Bill entered the car in the Top Dragster class and made it all the way to the final where he came up against the mighty 'Revolution' dragster of Clive Skilton. Two weeks earlier Clive had become the first Brit to go into the sevens and had repeated the feat at this meeting. Bill was desperate to beat Clive and, for the first time, appeared in a full fire suit and mask. The reason for this was apparently that he had upped the nitro content of his fuel quite considerably. The gamble didn't pay off however as he pulled a red light and a huge wheelie before shutting off to a losing 11.26/137.74 to Clive's 7.86/136. Bill did manage to take the NDRC Championship points title and the Top Dragster crown. He took top honours at almost every BDR&HRA and NDRC meeting and set a new World Speed Record for the Standing Start 500 metres at 10.12/120.6mph. He also set the flying 500m record at 185mph. Incidentally Bill's crew included three brothers called Page, Dave and Gary, who would go on to make their own mark on UK Drag Racing in the years to come.

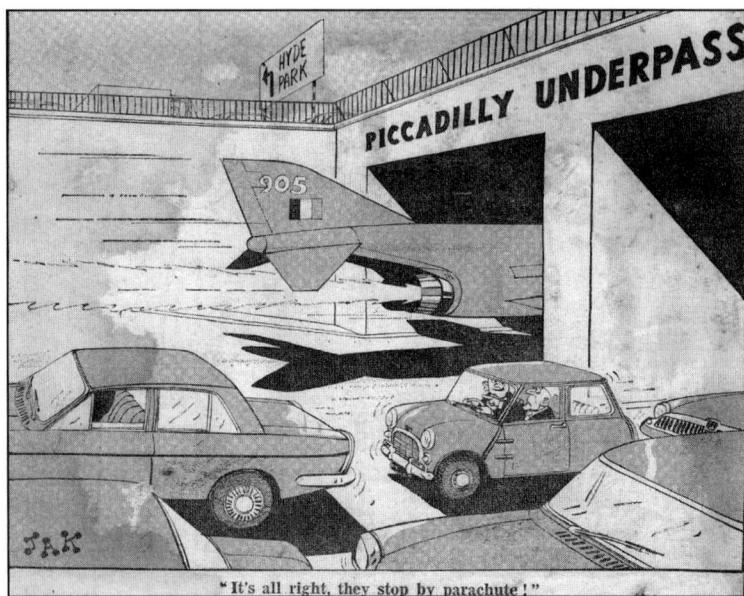

"It's all right, they stop by parachute!"

The car also featured in an advertising film alongside Nobby Hills Houndog exiting from London's Piccadilly underpass!

1970 ...

Dave Lee Travis (DLT), the beginning of a friendship and common interest in drag racing

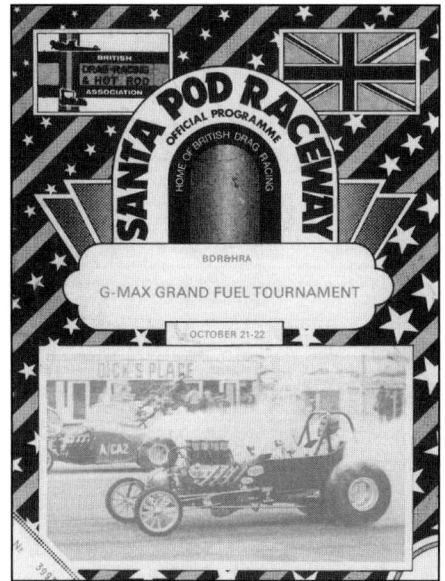

I first met Dave Lee Travis (DLT) in 1970 at the Drag Racing Christmas Party. at the Strathmore Hotel, Luton. At that time he was 'The Hairy Monster Road Show'. It soon became apparent we shared a very common interest in drag racing and racing cars.

From that time on we always met at the race track at Santa Pod. At that time he raced a Pontiac which was a street car. He always showed a lot of interest in my cars. One day he came up there with a video camera, it was the first one I had ever seen, he was able to film my car and show it to us on his television which he kept in his camper van.

Tender Trap

From then on he moved over from his street car to driving 'Tender Trap' which was a Stones car belonging to the Stones family. I used to go to the start line with him and give him my honest opinion on his reaction times to the lights.

Dave Lee Travis and his wife Marianne, were regulars at our Saturday night barbecues. They were a popular event possibly because it became known I always lit the barbecue with nitro methane! Marianne, being Swedish was a great help to me as she translated many Swedish

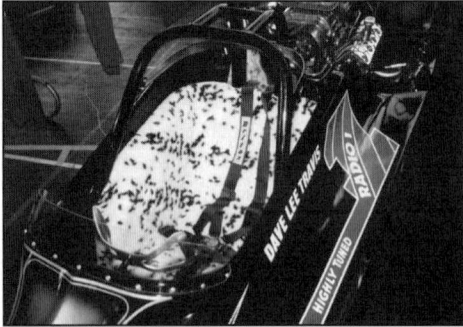

DLT's 'Needle' – top fuel dragster

drag racing magazines into English for me.

I was able to discuss with DLT on many occasions the building of my new rear engine dragster. This was the Houndog that was later purchased by Santa Pod and modified by Roy Phelps and Alan Herridge to become the Needle which Dave Lee Travis eventually drove to a 6.6 second and a speed of 230mph.

Our friendship continued over the years and he became firm friends with my wife Anne and little daughter Jodie who was born in 1978. She always enjoyed wearing his headphones. He called her "the happiest baby in the world" and he was a great comfort to us sadly when Jodie died in a road accident in her twenties.

Anne and Jodie looking at DLT who made her smile

1971 ...

Disaster the death of a Houndog!!!

On the 19th April of this year the Houndog achieved 9.7 sec run at 137 mph. Then after that came more changes, namely a new Piper cam, custom built for the car, a Scheifer clutch and Goodyear slicks.

However we then had a major setback in the form of a 130mph entanglement with the Santa Pod crash barriers on May 16th. It was caused by the failure of a slick on a 9.84 run. Mike was okay but shaken, and sadly the Houndog sustained heavy damage. Mike was about to pull the chute after a 137.36 mph win against the Glo Worm Capri funny car driven by Alan Herridge.The article Colour it Smokey portrayed the accident and helped us announce our plans for 1972.

Results of the collision with the Santa Pod barrier after a tyre blow out!

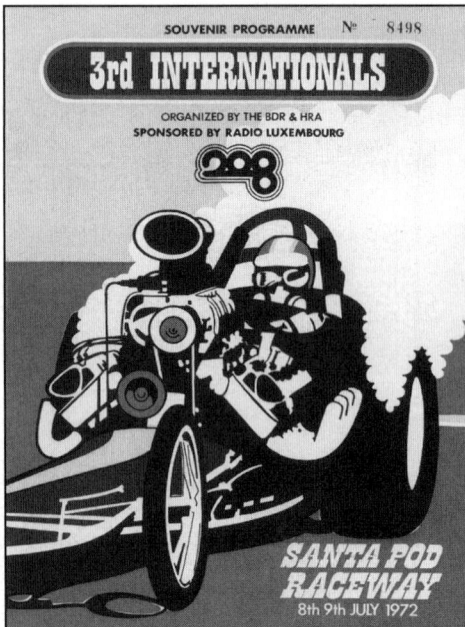

Colour it Smokey

*W*hen Movin' Mike Hutcherson suffered a tyre collapse that led to a 130mph crash with Santa Pod's crash barriers last May most people thought that Nobby Hills team would abandon the big fuel dragster ranks and maybe think in terms of a funny car for 1972. Their Cadillac powered Houndog fueller was a total write-off (though we gather the motor has since been acquired by a bunch of guys with TVR connections), and with the sort of investment needed to build an all-new car many people accepted the fact that Britain was now down to four double-A diggers.

But not Nobby Hills. As he surveyed the wreckage – driver Mike Hutcherson thankfully was little more than shaken – plans were taking shape in the part of his anatomy normally covered by a big Stetson and by the end of the week Nobby was excitedly outlining the plot for 1972. A better car, a faster car, and of course, a longer car.

Said Nobby: "we're gonna build a Hemi Chrysler that will knock them out".

Chrysler block

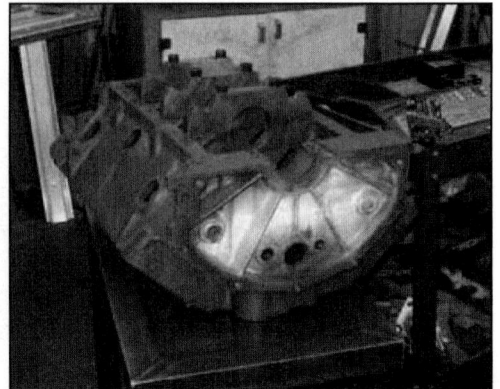

1972 ...

Nine months work – Houndog 5 here we come

We did it. One hundred and ninety-eight inches wheel to wheel, Chrysler powered and beautiful.

Thanks to the assistance from virtually all areas of the sport, mainly Santa Pod Raceway and Kelly-Springfield tyres, we were able to nail together some of the best quality hardware available. I built this after buying a Marine 354 Hemi in a box, this was brand new, the other parts I added were supplied by Bob and Roy Phelps of FGR.

Packed full of super-trick goodies such as Venolia pistons and rings, Mickey Thompson rods, an Isky 550 Magnum bumpstick, Federal-Mogul bearings, Keith Black valves and headers and a Schiefer clutch.

The block is a 1957 Dodge 354-cuber (5.8 litres) punched out to 5.9 litres, with a stock Mopar crank. As I wanted this beast to run in the eight-second bracket without straining the motor, I decided to run it soft on methanol with perhaps a whiff of nitro.

The juice is fed through a moon-ised 6/71 huffer with Hilborn injection mounted on a Weiand manifold, with a set of Auto-lite plugs lighting the fire. Compression ratio is 6:1.

Alan Herridge worked with me on the front axle construction, producing the front hubs and wheels which feature Avon rubber. The front spindles were modified Ford units, while the steering was

based around a BMC box.

The car was debuted at the Custom Car Show in February with its drum rear brakes, but because of a new BDR & HRA regulation calling for discs to be fitted on new diggers it meant that the new Houndog had to wear a new pair of stoppers for the strip.

It took us nine months and £2000 investment to get going again but we did it. This car was the fastest in the UK in 1972 with 179 mph 8.1 secs.

Hills-Hutcherson "Houndog" takes top spot!

The car was also declared the best exhibit at the Custom Car Show in London in 1972. In that year the timing ticket for the 29th May shows a run of 9.02 at 168.07 mph.

Early stages of Houndog 5 body panels, at a trial fitting stage. Below end of another run

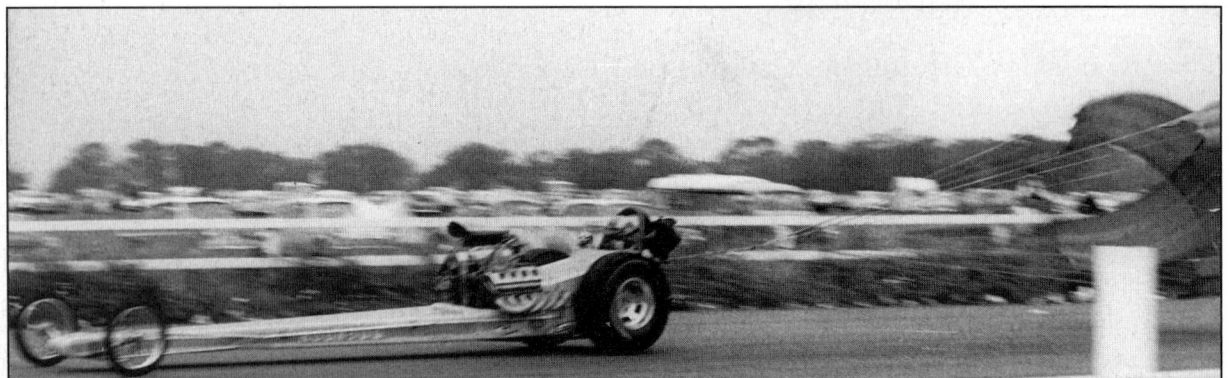

1973 update ...

Houndog 6 – new colours

Houndog 6 – again built on another chassis using lots of the running gear and increased the motor to the dream motor of the time – a 392. This was an immediate successful runner. It won runner up awards as the best dragster and the runner up award for the best overall competition machine at the Custom Car Show.

With an ex Firefly 392 Hemi engine and a new metal flake paint job it was really an eye catching car and I was very proud of myself and the team with it.

On one of the drag race report cards it was shown to have a top speed of 196.08 mph at 7.52 which was an incredible achievement.

Above and below: the big Hemi making more smoke!

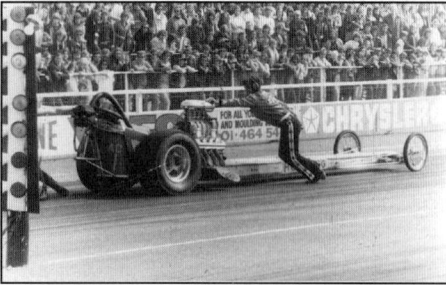

During the 1973 Santa Pod International the Houndog took on Tony Nancy's 470 cu in rear mounted Hemi engineered dragster. Mike tried hard to get a hole shot over Tony Nancy and pulled a giant wheelie for 50 yards up the track. He kept his foot in hard and a 7.7 seconds against Tony Nancy's 6.69 run at 213 mph.

On October 21st 1973 we won the Drag Racing News Trophy for the fastest speed near 230 mph – the speed actually reached a tremendous 163 mph. Unfortunately the engine has a suspect cracked block. We also came up against Dennis Priddle but again had more problems when the rear axle broke.

Movin Mike taking it easy

NOBBY'S QUARTER MILE

At the Annual 1973 Fireworks Meeting it was raining. On the Saturday evening of the two day meeting Mike Hutcherson was wheeled down in the Houndog for a fire burnout, much to the delight of the many spectators. The Sunday evening, whilst sheltering under the awning of the Houndog trailer, we heard an announcement that Mike was to do another demonstration fire burnout. "That's news to me" he said but then he got into the car and was pushed down the fire road. He then performed the fire burnout to end all fire burnouts. With such a spectacular bolt of flame he managed to set fire to the roof of the spectators barn and most of the staging area!!!

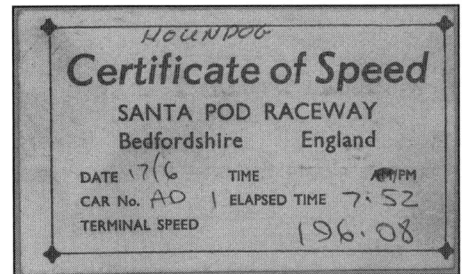

HOUNDOG
Certificate of Speed
SANTA POD RACEWAY
Bedfordshire   England
DATE 17(6   TIME   AM/PM
CAR No. AO   ELAPSED TIME 7:52
TERMINAL SPEED   196.08

Peter Billinton has the best seat in the house! In the background a young Owen Hayward

Nobby and Anne

In 1973 ...

I met Anne my lovely wife

This was a very good year for many reasons but the main one being it was the year that Anne and I met. She worked at SLD Olding as a personal secretary to the then Commercial Director, who bought her down to the main workshop where I was working on the top fuel dragster at the time. She has always had a great interest in cars so I was very lucky and our relationship progressed from there, and from that day she has always been totally supportive of my drag racing projects and thankfully still is.

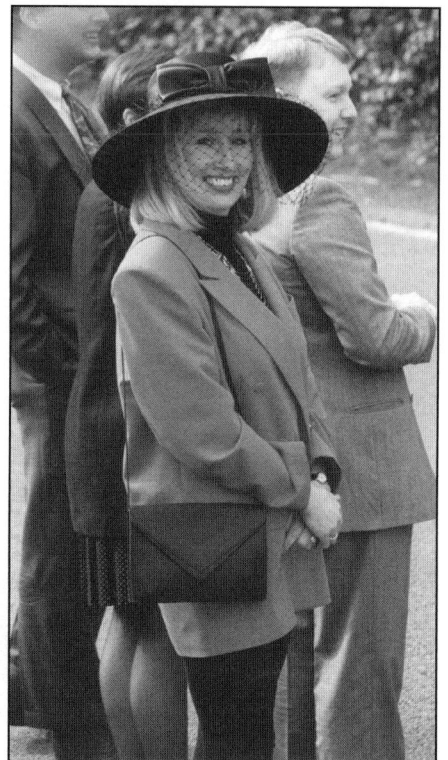

Something different for 1973

Houndog 7 – a Funny Car

Remembering back to 1972 when I went to the Summer Nationals Englishtown, New Jersey and saw American Funny Cars, it was fantastic and I was lucky enough to watch the STP funny car of Paula Murphy. I believe there was a field of 32 cars running, I loved each and every one of them. I had no idea then that within a few years the STP car would be mine wasn't I lucky!

Leading on to 1973 Internationals a Funny Car was brought over by Paula Murphy to match race the Stardust Car owned and run by Don Schumacher.

I was very interested in this kind of car as it looked possibly more like a saloon car to the average spectator as opposed to the elongated shape of a top fuel dragster.

My orders were to stick as close as I could to Paula's mechanic Fat Jack Bynum and her and the STP car, as this was to become the Houndog 7 Funny Car. This was precisely why I wanted I learnt so much about drag racing, particularly the elephant motors of the day. I was with the team the whole time they were operating in the UK, it was just a fantastic time for me. I tried very hard to take everything in that I was being shown, I remember Don Schumacher who was over with the Stardust Funny, saying that he was going to do a fire burnout. This sounds good, "tell me all about it Jack" (Bynum) and he did! He said we needed to remove as much rubber from the underside of the body and the tin work as we can; he explained with the build up of the rubber and traction compound it is more than likely it will catch fire, so you can guess what my job was for the next hour.

Off we go to the start line area, the usual routine was followed and both cars were fired up, then we put down the secret weapon, the propylene oxide which was put down where the water would normally go on the track. Don Schumacher moved violently forward and wow what a sight, the first fire burnout at Santa Pod raceway had just occurred. Paula moved forward with the Duster doing a long smokey burnout, unfortunately no fire burnout for her. Jack commented that there was not enough propylene to do two fire burnouts, what a pity! As you all probably know we made up for this on many occasions when Owen was driving the cars.

The specifications on this were a Plymouth Duster replica body with a Kent Fuller and Romeo Palamedies chassis of chrome molybdenum. It had a 124 inch wheel base, the front track is 47 inch and the rear track is 40 inch. The engine was an Ed Pink Nodular iron block based on the Chrysler 426. It had a forged stroker crank with pink rods holding 4¼in flat top button pistons, stock head and inlet valves and Donovan headers and rocker gear, Brown Brothers push rods and cam shaft and 6.71 teflon sealed Cragar blower at a 46% overdrive. It had a 3 port Enderle bug catcher and Enderle injection. A magneto 72° in advance. The plugs were Champion N60s except one cylinder which had an N57 as I felt it ran a bit hot. The car used STP with the oil, it had a Crowerglide triple plate slipper clutch, Lakewood bell housing, Lenco 2 speed and reverser, and Lenco/Ford axle. Rear end ratio was 3.9:1, the 2 speed ratios were 1.57:1 and 1:1. It had Cragar magnesium alloy wheels with 4.40 x 17 front tyres and rear slicks

16 x 16 x 36. The bumps were smoothed out by a Kent Fuller torsion bar at the front. There were two 12 inch Airheart disc brakes backed up by twin Diest parachutes. The brake horsepower was about 1,900 using 90% nitro methane.

We decided this car would be driven by Owen Hayward (he was already one of the crew with minimal experience but when it came to it he really took to this much envied position with a natural aptitude for the drive).

When it was tried out it reached runs of 8.8 secs at 187mph. But by the end of the season with our gained experience the car produced enormous burnouts to thrill the crowds and on one run recorded 7.43 secs at 167.79mph. We all felt this was good progress for a car of this different type and for half a season.

Madeira Drive, Brighton

NOBBY'S QUARTER MILE

For me personally 1973 was possibly one of my greatest years in drag racing. I was busy running the Duster and drawing the rear engine fuel dragster chassis and body. I had recorded 44 passes with the top fuel and Funny Car in this single year. I still say to this day when I look back at my many records I must admit I had fantastic support from SLD Olding and Santa Pod Raceway that made all this possible.

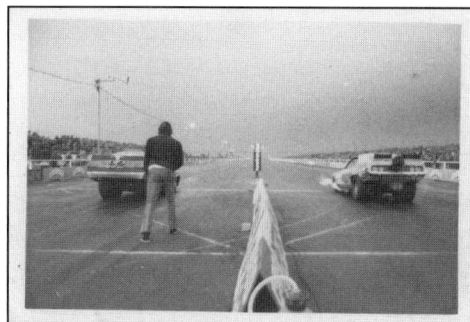

One hiccup that perhaps we should prefer not to remember I was working closely with Santa Pod at that time and I towed Dave Watts in the SPR Transit down to Bromley one evening in the week from SPR. There was a problem with the engine but anyway everything was fine until we reached a roundabout in South London. When I stopped he let the transit come up really close to the rear of my Pontiac. I did not notice when I pulled away and there was a big jolt. At the end

Drag racing at it best!

Lee Anders Hasselstrom

Hasse Fromme

of it the transit finished up facing the wrong way beside the Pontiac with a Belicia Beacon bent over about thirty degrees and the light still flashing, fortunately no other damage!

I met many famous drag racing people at this time including Ragnor Segrin, who helped organise and get the Duster for its first Scandinavian outing at Mantorp Park in Sweden. Ragnor was the Race Director for the whole complex. While at Mantorp Park I met another Funny Car Racer, Hasse Fromme, running his funny car Ragnarok. Also Lee Anders Hasselstrom who sadly many years later was killed in a horrific funny car fire. All great people.

Alan Bates and Nobby – happy days

We caught up with Paula Murphy who still lives in California ...

Here she gives us her account of 1973 with memories of England, drag racing and Nobby

In June 1973 I was invited to bring my Miss STP Plymouth Duster to race in England. Along with my crew, Jack Bynum and Rob Schlorer, we were really delighted to be asked to come over for three weekends of racing, two weekends at Santa Pod and one at the HMS Daedalus. Unfortunately we were rained off that weekend. But the other two weekends at Santa Pod had lots of sunshine and great fans. One of those fans was Nobby, who had been selected to take the car over when we returned to California. I even had my own private dressing room in Nobby's trailer to get in and out of my fire suit.

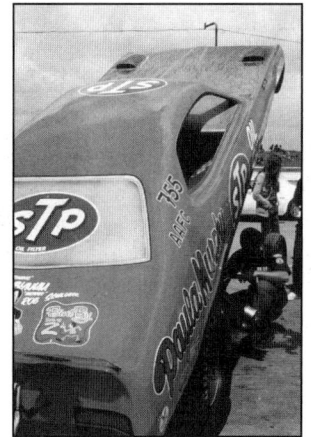

Paula Murphy

It has been a long time since we were at Santa Pod, but some things I remember: no iced cold drinks – so I then bought a big scoop of vanilla ice cream and poured my Coke into the ice

PAULA MURPHY--America's fastest girl drag racer is campaigning the "Miss STP Oil Treatment Special" on the nation's drag strips this season. The supercharged, 1500-hp Plymouth "Duster" is capable of speeds faster than 200 mph in a quarter-mile run.

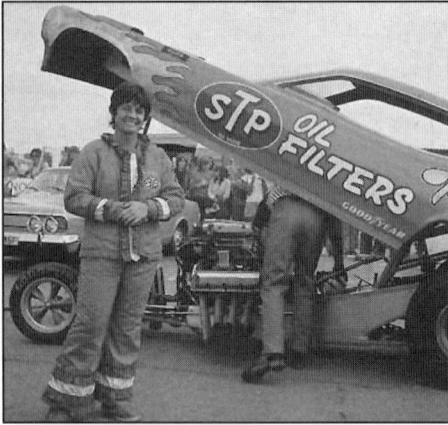

Paula in her fire suit

Jack Bynum mechanic

cream. We didn't have any cold beer at the hotel we stayed at but convinced the bartender to put some in the fridge for us. My mechanic Jack, pulled a big stunt, unbeknown to me, and had me do a fire burnout (which I had never done before). I think the fans loved it.

I have since been back to England and found that the Brits have learned to serve some of their beverages ice cold. Driving on the "wrong side" of the street and the driver sitting on the "wrong" side of the car was challenging, to say the least. The roundabouts were fun. Next time I come over, I am going to make a sign to put in the back window of my rental car that reads, "Caution American Woman Driver". Tony Nancy, who brought his top fuel dragster to Santa Pod with us, refused to drive on the streets.

I certainly loved coming to England and meeting so many welcoming people. Nobby has sent me his press kit with pictures of his gorgeous new Funny Car. Looks like it will be very successful and I wish him the best of luck and lots of race wins. I miss my old car, but it found a good home with Nobby.

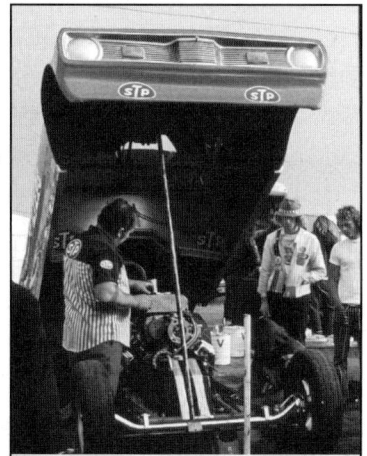

Paula.

Nobby says: I asked Paula if she would like a coffee, white or black? She replied coffeemate please, and I had to ask what coffeemate was? At that time of course coffeemate had not arrived in Great Britain.

1974 ...

Houndog 7 – wheelie record

The 1974 season also went well for this car as it progressed to lower E.T.s and low sixes. At the 1974 Custom Car Show the Houndog got its new colour and we officially called it Houndog 7. The paintwork involved quite complicated feathering, fogging and metal flake finishes superimposed over an overall pattern of blue on white panels which on the background colour of metal flaked red made a really fantastic look. John Harpum was responsible for this brilliant paint job at F.G.R.

Nobby concentrating

After having performed for the Santa Pod TV advert and running qualifying runs for the Super Nationals on August 25/26 1974 elimination day dawned and Owen Hayward was in competition against Dennis Priddle in his Avenger Funny. The psyche work began as the Funnies both did double burnouts, the traction was excellent and the Houndog was loaded for a hoped 6 run. Both cars blasted off on the go but from the line the Houndog started on a wheelie that will never be equalled! Still ahead of Priddle, Owen kept his boot in until the wheelie got to the stage that all four wheels were off the ground and the car was standing on the moulded rear bumper and virtually vertical! Owen brought the car down still under power, shut off and stopped at about the two thirds mark. The crash crews screamed up the strip and a cheer of relief erupted from the crowds as Owen climbed out from the car unhurt but he did suffer from slight altitude sickness.

See the explanation of this in the **Nobby Hills profile on page 112.**

10 years ...
of drag racing for
Nobby Hills

How time flies we had now been involved, and very successfully at that, with drag racing for 10 years. Now running a top fuel dragster, the Houndog 6 and the Funny Car, the Houndog 7.

Another highlight of the era was the crew being awarded the Kelly Springfield Cup for 1973 for the unending efforts to further the sport of drag racing.

Here is the Nobby Hills profile that summarises nicely the ten years so far. It is taken from a drag racing magazine. The interview was conducted by a PH.

NOBBY HILLS PROFILE

Nobby Hills, *the man whose trade marks are consistency, friendliness and a pair of cowboy boots and flip flops.*

(Just for the record I had taken to wearing flips flops on the track as I found them very comfortable!)

PH: How did it start for you Nobby?

NH: Initially back in 1959, I started buying Hot Rod magazines and there were pictures of cars, hot rods, dragster or whatever, with smoke pouring off the tyres. Not only that, but they were still doing it 40 yards later. That, I thought, is different. So different that it fascinated me, so that when in 1963 I saw a tiny ad in the Sketch reading 'American dragster demonstrates at Silverstone tomorrow', I did no more than go up there and lo and behold, there was 'Mooneyes'.

Houndog 2

I bit it bad and it bit me worse and that was that. So, plans were laid for our first car, which was powered by gas in a blown 3.4 Jag. A the first meeting of the 1964 Fests we ran a 22.0 at 64mph for a start and that brought us back to earth with a bump and dispelled the hopes of running 150mph.

The second weekend we switched to alky and ended up with a 14.4 at 109 mph and in that race we gave Alan Herridge a good run for the money, just being beaten with a 14.2 in the final.

That was the first time I met Alan and we got chatting and I suppose we have been chatting ever since.

After that came another blown 3.5 Jag which gave us 11s and then the Caddy came along which gave us 9s. 9.9 with the 331 then came a 372 and a 9.6 before it wrapped itself into a wall. That was racing FGRs Capri bodied 'Gloworm'. Then came the Chrysler and that's about it to date.

PH: Who do you see as your biggest threat in T/F or F/C?

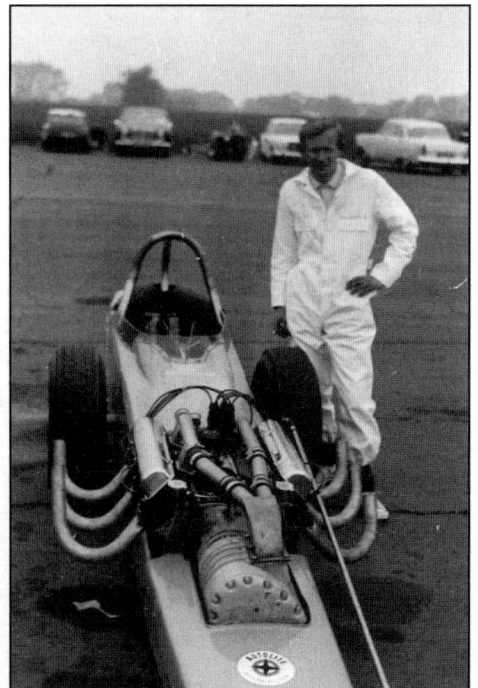

NH: Well I think Dennis is obviously still going to be the one to beat this year in top fuel, but a car that will really come on in 1975 will be 'Stormbringer'. That I feel is really going to change this year.

I think when you talk about threats, our car is a little heavy as against the American built cars, but what I'll say is that it will probably live longer, chassis wise, than the American cars, at the Pod, because it's simply been made to run that particular surface.

PH: Is this because of the infamous bumps in it?

NH: Yes. Our chassis work is a little bit heavier, larger tubing, than it really ought to be, but it will probably live longer because of that. That may also make it a slightly bit more slower, which is why I say it'll run, well in my opinion, a 6.7 and I think it will be limited around that sort of range.

PH: What about the Funny Car field?

NH: Quite honestly, I don't think there's anything to touch us if we can get it all together and that's the honest truth. Ours is the latest car in the country, apart from Dennis's, but his, well I'll just say ours is a better car.

No, I don't think anything will touch us, whatever they do to Stardust for it's the heavier car no matter what anybody says.

PH: What about the two drivers though? Do you think that given the, in your opinion, lesser car, Alan will outdrive Owen?

NH: Yes, if it were true, but Owen is the better driver altogether, but the season will tell, come and see me again at the end of it!

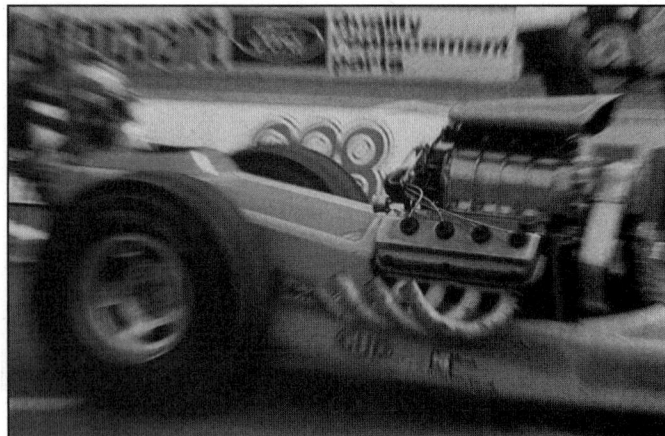

PH: So what are your plans for 1975 then?

NH: Simply to run harder and faster than anyone else, I hope. We want to see the Funny Car running consistently in the sixes and I would like to see the Dragster get down to the 6.7s, though as I said, this will probably be its full potential.

PH: What do the tickets read at the moment?

NH: Well for the Dragster, it's 6.96 at 198mph and the Funny Car is 6.76 at 202mph.

PH: Well you are about to enter your 11th year as an owner/builder, how do you see the future?

NH: As it stands I reckon, it's going to be one of the biggest motor sports in the country, but I can see it taking an awful long time, a long long time like everything does in this country. I think may be as we get a few more big burners, or fuel cars, on the strip, people will always come back to see them. I would love to see all the country's top cars running at the Pod as it is obviously the best facility that there is, anybody, that's anybody, who runs a good time, runs there and I think it's the place to run.

PH: So can you see any improvements you would like to make to the sport?

NH: The main one is, I feel, to get everybody running together or against each other at Santa Pod. A lot of people have put a lot of effort into creating a good facility, it is new and if everybody got together and made a show and advertised it as such, I think that is the single biggest improvement that could be made.

PH: So would you like to see more co-operation between the two promoters?

N.H. You could say that, but I feel its a matter of using the best facility outside of America, which is the Pod. I know I keep on about the Pod, but the fact is that the best facility is afforded there and I do not see why anyone should want to drag people away anywhere else.

Quite simply Dennis and Clive, whenever they have run their good times, it has been at the Pod and they know as well as anybody else that it is the best strip about.

PH: Going back now to the Internationals the year before last, what were your feelings when the Pod asked you to run the second Funny Car for them?

NH: Astounded and overwhelmed sums it all up. After being in drag racing for so long and then seeing the Funny Cars and trying to believe them and then being offered the opportunity to have a go at running one was the biggest single thing that happened to me in racing.

Having all the best gear in it and all, it was a bit of an honour.

PH: What is your opinion of Paula's mechanic Jack Bynum?

I thought he was the most fantastic mechanic you could ever hope to find. He just knew everything, I mean that.

There was nothing about Funny Cars that man did not know about and that is a fact.

PH: That gigantic wheelie of Owen's last year, the biggest in Europe, must have put years on both of you. What happened?

NH: Well that, though I'm not proud of it, was entirely down to me. We worked a little bit backwards on the clutch and found the traction and gradually bought the clutch back to where it ought to be. On the last adjustment I overdid it and put a little too much stall on it and let the engine get into its torque range and obviously there is nothing going to stop one of these motors when it wants to go. It just happened that we also found the most traction that was about on the strip at that meeting and of course the clutch locked up with the surface and as Owen said, normally when he shifts into second it drops back down on the front wheels. This time it just kept going up and up and up. He said when he couldn't see anything but blue sky he shut the fuel off (quiet chuckle!) Yes, terrific!

PH: What were you feeling at the time?

NH: Well to be honest, I didn't know I honestly thought we had lost the car! I think one of the reasons we came off so lightly was down to the driver. He was running straight and true, it went up straight and came down more or less straight in the centre of the spectator lane. Obviously it wrecked the front suspension but he was able to control the car and bring it to a standstill safely. So after putting in about 30 hours work it was repaired.

PH: So considering what happened the damage was light?

NH: Well, it was a lot but only superficial. Chassis, front suspension, body and the sump. The motor and all the other parts that cost money were all okay.

PH: It has been suggested that because your car and Stardust are both Pod owned, there is no inclination to run hard between you. What do you say?

NH: No, it is just not true. One of our main aims this year is to make Stardust run second, of that there is no doubt. I think Alan would agree that he has got to get his finger out and keep it out. As soon as the traction is there, they will run second, no doubt about it.

PH: Running two top class cars must take a hell of a lot of time. How much do you reckon you do in a week?

NH: I should say in the region of 20 hours a week. Having the cars where we work induces Owen and I to put the most in, at lunch times as well as in the evenings and the rest of the crew work about 6-10 hours. We get on the phone and say we are working tonight and manage that way.

PH: Who are the crew this year?

This year Owen is driving both cars, then there is myself, big Alec and young Alan and that is it.

PH: I believe there was some talk when you got the Funny Car, of you driving, what happened?

NH: You can't get 6ft4in into 4ft6in! No the reason was I tried it out for size and found when I had my helmet on it came between the two main tubes of the roll cage, so it was much too small for me. I would like to have driven it and one day I'll have a little go in it just to see what it is like. I had a go in all the other cars bar the Chrysler engined cars and I've no inclination to drive the rail. Having built them up I tend to visualise all the nuts and bolts going round and .... well not for me!

Disaster ...

of Houndog 6

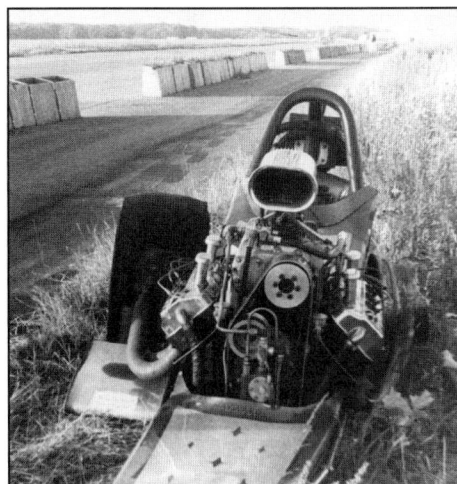

Disaster struck us on the day of the debut of Houndog 8 in regard to the Houndog 6. The car had been sold to Santa Pod Raceway after being advertised at the Pod and in the Exchange and Mart for £1600.

Unfortunately in the hands of Harold Bull, of Stripbuster fame, on only his second run the Houndog was driven to destruction. Oil leaked from one of the rocker covers as the Houndog went through the timing taps.

Harold Bull was unable to see where he was going and lost control of the car, the chute did not deploy, and the car veered over the left hand lane and crashed into the left hand crash barrier which consisted of boxes filled with lumps of concrete. The Houndog sadly was a total write off with the exception of the engine.

It is hard to describe the sorrow the whole team felt for the car had been a faithful friend and we all remembered those nights we had spent in the murky depths of the Santa Pod hangers welding up the axle after major strip downs.

What follows is how this was reported in the supporters club newsletter 21st July 1974.

The Life and Death ...
of a Houndog

I must now tell you about the death of a Houndog. The Houndog in question is Nobby's old rail which was bought by Santa Pod Raceway at the Internationals. The dragster still carried the name Houndog although in time I suppose it would have been repainted and renamed. Harold Bull was put in the seat on Sunday and after making a trial run down the strip in the morning came out for a full timed blast down the quarter in the afternoon. After a very good burnout Harold staged the dragster with no fuss, waited for the green and then took off on a beautiful full pass recording 8.15 ET. 189 T.S. Just after Harold had gone through the top end he was suddenly blinded by a jet of oil. Instinct told him to pull the chute and although it came out it never deployed and the car veered left, going from the spectator lane to the pit lane and hitting the crash boxes in the braking area. Although braking hard as the skid marks showed later, the car was still travelling fast and the force of the impact smashed the front left hand wheel and slick and completely bent the frame.

Luckily Harold escaped with bruised legs and a bitten tongue. No one weld on the frame was broken which says a lot for Nobby's construction and welding, but the car was so twisted that it will never race again. Looking at the wreckage made me feel very sad because that old Houndog had given me, and other, many hours of pleasure, win or lose she always came back.

Thanks all for now. See ya at the Pod. John Lees.

1974 ...

The debut of Houndog 8 – top fuel rail

What a great day July 21st 1974 for the Houndog team, the Houndog Supporters Club and the majority of the spectators who crowded into the pits to see the unveiling of the new rear engined Houndog 8 – sometimes referred to in the press as The Rail.

This time the car was based on a Tony Nancy design and it took us the first half of the year to construct this car.

Painted in a similar style to the Funny Car there was a great deal of tension as the car was pulled out of the famous Houndog trailer.

The car was then pushed down the fire up road. Mike soon got used to the handling and it went round the bottom corner and drove up into the pre-staging area for the burnout. Mike then executed a magnificent burnout with thick white smoke curling round the wheels, he burned over the line and stopped.

Stu Bradbury, Santa Pod's then start line official, walked up to the front of the car ready to push it back, Mike waved his hand and said, "get off, go away!" He then pushed a lever and the car backed slowly into the staging area.

Houndog 8 was the first pro fuel dragster to have a reverser fitted! He then pulled up to stage, the lights rolled down and he ran a quarter try out pass at 12.2 seconds. Some hours later after resetting up the clutch and checking out the engine and chassis, the car again came down the fire road, this time he appeared to be running in competition as he was against Bootsie Herridge in Firefly. The cars then proceeded to execute the ritual burnouts across the line, they both came into stage, the lights rolled down and Mike was off like a rocket on the green pulling in an enormous hole shot over Firefly. With only a half pass he ran at 7.3 seconds with Firefly trailing all the way, in fact Bootsie Herridge succeeded in blowing his engine to pieces in trying to catch Mike in the new Houndog – what a brilliant start we had to this vehicle, we were all pretty pleased with ourselves.

Mike justifiably got the top fuel trophy and the crowds were really appreciative. We then put the car away to carry out checks and modifications as we always did on the new runouts.

After running the 6.96 ET this now made Mike Hutcherson the fourth non-American to run under the then magical seven second barrier.

Soon after the success of this car, we had changes with drivers. It was around this time that Mike left the crew and Owen, another SLD Olding's nitro burning employee like myself, already the

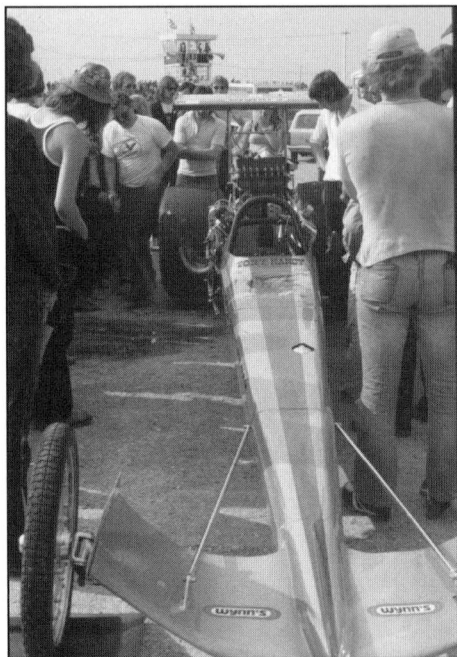

driver of the Funny Car, took over as driver of both cars.

See press mention:

Top fuel saw a couple of driver changes. In addition to the Houndog Funny, Owen Hayward is now handling the team's digger, Mike Hutcherson having parted company with the team. His first run was a very credible 7.7 – and they say he'd never sat in a fueller before! A cracked block unfortunately put the car out of action for the day.

Not only did the April meet see a new low-ET mark in this country for Top Fuel cars (previous best was Pete Crane's 6.37 put down at Easter), but the Funny Car ranks now have a new king in Houndog driver Owen Hayward. The pastel-coloured Duster campaigned by Nobby Hills and his merry men became the quickest European fender flapper (by BDR & HRA clocks) turning 6.76secs, 185 mph after many months in the lower sevens!

More complimentary press mentions for our team:

213 mph HOUNDOG

Since 1972 Nobby Hills racing team with Owen Hayward success on the drag strip has been unequalled on this side of the Atlantic.

In mid 1973 Nobby and Owen took over an American built 'Funny Car' to compliment their by now very strong running pro-fuel dragster. The Funny Car, which Owen drives, is anything but funny when it comes to accelerating through the quarter mile. The specially built Ed Pink Chrysler 484 cu.in. (8 litre) engine hauls the car from 0-100 mph in a staggering two and a half seconds.

A quarter mile, five gallons of nitro methane and seven seconds later, the car is travelling at over 200 mph (320 kph). Twin 14 foot parachutes slow the car down initially and massive disc brakes acting on the 16inch wide rear tyres bring the car to a standstill at the end of each run.

At the end of 1973 in a determined effort to 'stay out front' Nobby set about building a completely new dragster following the latest trend towards rear engine cars. Transmitting the power through a two speed 'power shift' box to the giant Goodyear racing slicks the supercharged nitro burning Chrysler engine pushed the new car back into the six seconds bracket.

On the 20th April 1974 with the help of an enthusiastic crew managed by Nobby, Owen officially broke the British and European 'Funny Car' record for the quickest elapsed time over the quarter mile setting a new all time low of 6.76 seconds. A terminal speed of 213 mph!!!!

Chutes out!

SUPPORTERS CLUB REPORT
21st JULY 1974

Dear Member,

Let's get straight down to the Houndog Race Report.

There was no Houndog funny car at this meeting as it was being prepared for its trip to Sweden but it was certainly the day of the Houndog as you will see.

9.30am Sunday morning and no sign of Nobby or Houndog but then round goes the word that Nobby and crew are on the way from Hatfield with Houndog 8, yes folks the new rail was coming out. Soon afterwards up rolled Nobby, opened the boot of his car and out came the wing for the rail – "don't worry" he said "the rest is coming". So there we all were waiting for the first signs of the trailer and after what seemed like hours it suddenly appeared and so did half the spectators. Nobby kept us all in suspense by only rolling out the back of Houndog 8 while he bolted on the wing but we could already see the gleaming chrome and paint and we knew then that all the months of waiting had been worthwhile.

For those of you who were not there I can only describe the paintwork as being nearly the same colours and design as the funny car, plus of course plenty of chrome. A lot of people said that the new rail looked short, well Nancy's rail was a bit shorter than say the Castrol dragster as Houndog was built to Tony Nancy's plans. Also the body panelling is higher than what we have been used to, so this also gives it a stubby effect. Anyway this

Club logo – Sloane and below Houndog T-Shirts

new Houndog is so good that it didn't have to go to the scrutineer, in fact the scrutineer came to Houndog. After a quick check over and a questions and answers session with Nobby, the new Houndog got the ticket and was passed with honours and the crew now got down to work.

The first test was on the rollers where it was fired up and checked out for oil pressure, etc. Then off the rollers still fired up Mike turned as far as possible in the confined space, reversed up (to the amazement of those people who were not in the

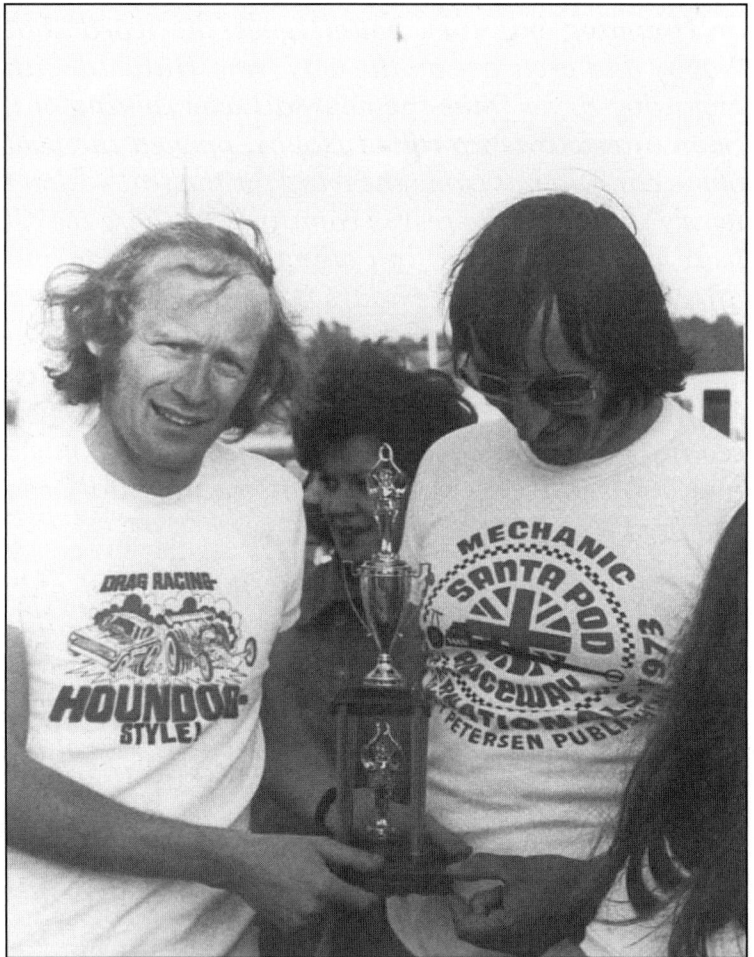

A very proud Mike and Nobby

know about Nobby's latest trick) and then put Houndog into forward gear and drove back to the pits.

Now it was down to the real test, would the new frame take the stress of a strong burnout and the power when coming off the line. Well there was only one way to find out and that was to go and do it. Down the fire up road came the Houndog, fired up and ready for the christening. Mike didn't quite make the turn first time but after a bit of juggling about got into the bleach area for the pit lane. Down went the bleach and then Mike let loose with a true Tony Nancy burnout with smoke completely covering the slicks and taking him further than his old burnouts. Into reverse again and this really had the spectators rubbing their eyes in disbelief, can that really be a pro fuel dragster going backwards under it own power, it sure is and Nobby Hills should make the headlines with that little trick.

Mike now brought Houndog into stage with a little help from Nobby's hand signals and we waited to see if the car would perform well off the line. On came the green and away she went dead straight and handling well, so Houndog had passed with flying colours. Only a blast off the line and then shut off but Mike still got a time ticket 12.06 E.T., 66.11 T.S.

Houndog was then declared ready for action and so it was decided to run a best of three against Firefly which was once again being driven by Bootsie as Pete Crane was still trying to get out of the knots he got into at the last meeting.

Down came Mike in Houndog choosing the pit lane and Firefly going over to the spectator lane, once again Mike having a bit of trouble with the turn but he will soon sort that out. Firefly burns out first

John and Brenda Lees who ran the Houndog International Supporters Club for many years

followed by Houndog, not quite as good as the first one but good enough. The Santa Pod crew heaved away at Firefly while Mike did it all himself and several spectators rushed off to the first aid for eye sight tests and mental checks. Mike getting carried away was about to reverse back up the fire up road until Nobby signals stop and then we see Nobby's funny car signals being given to Mike to bring him into stage. Both cars in stage, the ambers flickered down, two greens came on and "wow" Houndog rocketed off the line pulling a massive hole shot over Firefly and goes tearing off down the strip way out in front. Mike knew he had Firefly beaten and shut off by the tower. While Firefly was still thrashing away trying to catch up, the old Dodge engine decided to call it a day and let loose with a rod and spread the rest of the engine all over the track. Houndog's first competitive run was a winner, even shut off Houndog recorded 7.31 E.T. 158.73 T.S., Firefly losing out at 8.26 E.T. 130.72 T.S. With Firefly out of action Houndog was proclaimed pro fuel winner of the meeting and picked up the trophy just to prove it. The new Houndog is a dead certain six second runner so we shall soon see the top of the pile boys Skilton and Priddle come out to make a challenge I hope.

John Lees

Movin' Mike Hutcherson ...

We caught up with him and he tells us just how it was back then

My first taste of drag racing came at Blackbushe in 1964 – International Drag Fest – little did I know that drag racing was to become a major part of my life.

I met Nobby and the late Ron Doyle at Jack Oldings Ltd. where Nobby worked, at the time Nobby was looking for a new driver, when he heard I had previously done some test driving for LOTUS DEVELOPMENT he offered me the drive in Houndog 3 – first Caddy Powered Dragster.

I didn't need asking twice!

My first meeting was at Santa Pod in 1966 – the dragster looked great – although it did not run too well but it was a start. My first complete quarter mile was 14 secs at 120mph.

Being an engineer by trade, Nobby soon roped me in to do the machining – half shafts – aluminium pulleys for the supercharger – manifolds etc., etc. meaning many late nights moonlighting at work. Working in a machine shop I could prepare everything I needed during the day and go back to work while the night shift was on and make the parts we needed.

One Sunday afternoon at Oldings Nobby was painting the engine block a strange orange colour

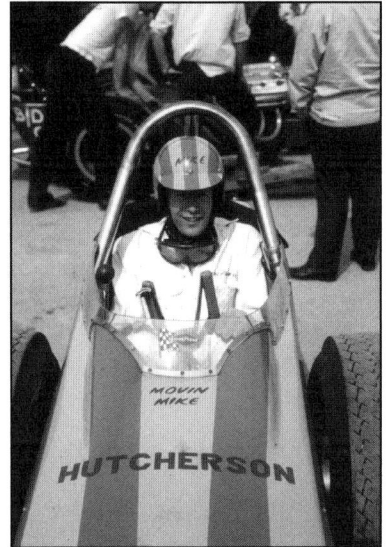

Mike Hutcherson at the wheel

– he asked me what I thought of the colour (being in awe of what was the most practical thinking man I have ever met), I said it's great – not wanting to criticise – at the time I didn't know Nobby was colour blind, hence the unusual colour of some of the cars!

In our efforts to develop more and more H.P. from the Caddies I lost count of the number of engines we broke. In 1969 a crisis meeting was held – Nobby had run out of money – we needed another V8 Caddy!

I had about £36 in the bank so I purchased an engine from the local scrapyard for £29 – like the vast majority of competitors with drag cars, we were normal working class blokes on normal wages – chipping in financially to share a bit of the expenses Nobby was paying out.

That was the last V8 Caddy we used, at the May meeting of 1971 I suffered a puncture in the nearside slick and wrecked the car against the safety barrier, a series of concrete filled boxes if I remember correctly. Typical of Nobby – he proudly announced to me that not one weld had broken on the car.

Back to the drawing board – building a new dragster (Houndog 5). A 354 cu in Dodge Hemi was obtained (with the help of Santa Pod Raceway) – we were going places. The new car was set up as a smoker – designed to spin the wheels all the way through the quarter (a la Garlits/Ivo at Blackbushe). Great car to drive – ran best 8.2 secs at 172 mph.

Houndog 5 had a lovely paint job and was runner-up for best exhibit at Custom Car Show in 1972.

Houndog 6 came next, same frame as a no. 5 – but

modified to take a 392 cu.in Hemi. Set up with a slider clutch – beautiful car to drive – (unusual paint colour), loved it, best ET 7.52 – 196 mph!

Everyone in the States was now running rear engined dragster – so guess what – Nobby wanted one – so off we go again. Houndog 8 was a spectacular looking dragster – I managed to break into the 6's a couple of times with this car. At this time Nobby acquired the ex Paula Murphy Funny Car and decided this was the way forward. He already had a driver for this car (Owen Hayward) so this seemed the proper time to retire.

I had enjoyed ten years of helping building and racing – so many memories – in the early days we would meet every Friday night at the Jolly Bargeman Pub in Ware to plan our campaign – every racing weekend would see us in the nearest pub to Santa Pod. Good times.

Our achievements included the advertisement for the Rover 2000 TC in all the papers. Filmed a commercial for Contrast Chocolates and filmed in the Piccadilly Underpass for a Italian film company as well as showing at Custom Car events, we even had a fan club, customised tee shirts (courtesy of my good friend Brian Williams (Little Will) photographer and man of many parts Brian Clark – very special thanks to Peter Hart who was with me in the team until 1974 – also the late Alex Brachtvogel who continued with Nobby after I retired also family support from my younger brothers David and Peter (Peter painted the Houndog on the side of the blue trailer).

Many thanks to Nobby who was the driving force behind everything we achieved. His single mindness and love of drag racing was second to none – a truly remarkable man – a genius in the world of drag racing.

Movin' Mike Hutcherson

Drag Racing:

Nobby Hills and the Houndog Team

by Brian E. Clark (who kindly supplied many of his photographs for this book)

Brian Clark

In 1969 my interest in cars and motor racing was steered to what is effectively the simplest form of a competitive motor sport (i.e. two cars competing to get to the end of a quarter mile first). It is, without doubt, the most spectacular form of racing, and is carried out by some of the most dedicated mechanical geniuses and car constructors you can find on the planet.

One such person is Nobby Hills. He is one of the guys who form the backbone of the sport.

My first vision of Mr. Hills was of a seven foot tall guy with a cowboy hat, American tee shirt, striped trousers (which were presumably made from deck chair fabric), and green and white flip-flops. He was scooping what appeared to be beige custard out of an engine sump into a large waste drum containing all sorts of spent automotive lubricants. I think from his rummaging about in the goo he was searching for a vital component lost within this jelly like mass.

"Who is that?" I asked the dragster driver, Mike Hutcherson, "Oh that's Nobby", he said, "he is in charge of the team, he builds the cars and we race them for him".

So began my long friendship with Mike and Nobby, together with Peter Hart, Alex Brachtvogel, Dave

and Alan Bates, Owen and Monica and the various other members of the Houndog and other teams.

Unlike some motor sports the drag racers community appears to go out of its way to help other teams despite being "rivals" on the strip. Nobby and the team were extremely friendly and approachable to spectators asking various questions, even when stress levels rose as the day became more hectic. Whilst methodically stripping down and re-building a motor between races Nobby and the team would explain what they were doing and the reason why. No Formula One style behind-the-scenes secrecy in dragster pits.

A Houndog Supporters Club, formed by John Lees, used to keenly follow the teams progress and would cheer them on as they competed. The Supporters "Fellowship" became a popular social part off the B.D.R. & H.R.A. meetings at the Pod. Houndog supporters included a contingent from Norfolk backed up by a strong Beds & Herts section who always arrived early on the first day of a weekend event. Our campsite of caravans and tents was located to the rear of the team's pit area and our evenings round the campfire were legendary.

Nobby would fire off his barbecue with nitromethane (because he could!) and we all sat around discussing important topics such as:

Does Nobby gauge his flip-flop adhesion to the track to evaluate traction compound deployment? The dubious merits of the Santa Pod loos (no plumbed water in those days).

We were known to have the odd beer or ten, some members even chancing the Norfolk boys' draft cider (which we also found suitable for rust removal or degreasing engines). The evening's entertainment was regularly enhanced by the sound of people falling into the ditch, which used to separate the pit area from he adjacent field, or in the early 70's watching the odd streaker running about (always an ugly bloke never a beautiful woman!)

The Supporters Club expanded rapidly and became International with the first Australian member (Frank) and later Paula Murphy was made its Honorary President. Many lasting friendships and some marriages were spawned within the membership of the Supporters Club.

You will have read elsewhere how The Houndog team gained publicity in various ways. At the first few meetings after watching Nobby and the team meticulously preparing and checking the dragster prior to its first run of the day. I would then find an appropriate vantage point to photograph the cars to produce pictures for some of the teams. Later on, with the endorsement of Nobby and Mike, I was in the position to carry out a P.R. role for the Houndog supporters and able to capture some spectacular runs of the cars and other drag racing events for publication in various magazines plus get some mention of Houndog on local and national radio stations. Nobby would introduce me to various key people involved in the sport; in particular guys who had started it all off in the early 60's at the Drag Fest events. Nobby lent me his precious scrap books and these together with various reports helped me compile a brief history of the first ten years of the Houndog for its supporters.

Nobby would enlist enthusiasts to help out with some of the simpler car preparations. My early

recollections include, polishing Houndog 6, meticulously highlighting the M&H name on the drag slicks with shoe whitening, driving down the fire-up road in the Buick powered 5.4 litre Cresta push car to push start the front engine dragster (Houndog 6), helping Dave Bates with the funny car (Houndog 7) clutch shims (see the story of the wheelie), and because I really admired the car so much volunteering to help polish Houndog 8.

Some Favourite Houndog Memories:

The B.D.R. & H.R.A. Dinner Dance at the Strathmore Hotel, Luton with DLT's Disco.

Remembering to take the pin out of the Dragster Chute pack on the start line.

The push car back axle breaking near the start line. It was welded up with no differential. Interesting to drive thereafter!

The sad demise of the Houndog 6 when Harold Bull crashed it.

Movin' Mike into the Sixes in the immaculate Houndog 8.

Buster the Wonderdog.

Nobby's Pontiac Parisienne.

Walnut Whip the Streaking Biker.

The relief seeing Owen was okay after the Houndog 7 funny car crash.

The Houndog Internatonal Supporters Club nights out at the Mile House, St. Albans (including Taffy's Burger Bar)!

A favourite recollection I have is seeing Nobby carrying out some chassis fabricating. Watching him welding is like observing an artist at work.

The man is totally dedicated to the sport yet has never driven a dragster in competition. As my great friend Movin' Mike Hutcherson had said to me nearly forty years previously "he builds them", "we race them".

Keep going Nobby "Quarter Star that's what you are"

Brian

Owen Hayward tells it all ...

Back in 1975 our driver Owen, then 27, gave an interview with Speed and Power magazine and told just how it was. Here is how it read ...

Howling Houndog 7

What's it like to blast down a dragstrip in a banshee howl of noise unleashed from a whopping 8 litre nitro-fuelled engine? Here Owen Hayward, driver of Houndog 7 Funny Car, puts you in the "hot seat" and tells you like it is!

Having almost 2,000 brake horsepower instantly available by merely pressing an accelerator with your right foot is a pretty frightening thought. But 27 year old Owen Hayward, driver of the Houndog team's Funny Car Dragster manages to stop as he catapults from a standstill to over 200mph in less than 7 seconds in his sleek 8,000cc engined machine.

The car, called Houndog 7, is one of the two top running cars campaigned by the team under the leadership of Nobby Hills, a production engineer from Ware, Hertfordshire. The second car runs in the out-and-out fuel dragster division and both are painted in matching colours of red, blue and white. But it is the fibreglass bodied Funny Car that we are going to take a "ride" in.

With so much power available it is not surprising that the car has set a best time of 6.76 seconds down the quarter mile, finishing with a speed of 214mph!

On one run the car actually reared up almost vertically half way down the track, with all four wheels lifting clear of the tarmac! Only the rear of the fibreglass body prevented it from going right over backwards!

In an effort to find out just what it is really like to hurtle down a dragstrip in such a short time, we asked Owen to tell Speed & Power readers what happens on a run, and the feelings he experiences.

Owen: With me firmly strapped into the seat, a portable starter is plugged into the supercharger drive shaft, and the engine started up after oil pressure has built up. Then the crew lower the body and lock it onto the chassis. I drive the machine to a suitable position just behind the start line, and a little water is laid under the rear slicks ready for the first of two burnouts, which will heat up the tyres and give more traction away from the start line. The car is then edged into the start light beams in a series of hops.

S&P: Why don't you just slip the clutch to come to the line?

Owen: Because the car has a centrifugally-operated clutch fitted. There is no clutch pedal, so I have to blip the throttle to "nudge" forward. If I revved up the car would take off!

S&P: What is it like as you power off the line on a run?

Owen: I can only say that it feels like I'm being launched in a rocket!

S&P: The sight and sound of two "funnies" tearing down the strip is an incredible spectacle – especially the sound. Are you aware of the noise from the motor?

Owen: Not really, it comes through as a very deep vibration rather than an ear-splitting sound.

S&P: How much can you actually see as you drive along the track?

Owen: All that is clearly visible from the start line is the finish, and I aim at a point in the middle of my lane past the finish line. As long as I can see that point then I'm heading in the right direction!

NOBBY'S QUARTER MILE

S&P: Some of your runs look rather hairy, especially when the wheels lift off. Does the car feel stable under acceleration?

Owen: It does tend to be a little unpredictable for the first half of the course, but I'm very happy with the stability at high speeds.

S&P: At 200mph stopping the car can't be easy. You must get quite a smack in the chest when the braking parachute is released?

Owen: I certainly do when I back off the throttle and pull the chute ring at the same time. Everything goes quiet for a brief period before a tremendous jerk slams me into the safety harness, which is kept very tight to avoid injury. Then it feels like I'm flying until the speed drops and the big discs start to bite. All I have to do then is wait for the support car to reach me and let me out!

And get him out we did!

The crew were very pleased to get Owen's experiences down in print as were the fans from the positive feedback we received when this went to press.

Owen speaks today ...

We have again caught up with Owen, and here in his own words he contributes more on both his early and later experiences and also his special friendship with Nobby

The two top fuel nitro burning Funny Cars that appeared at Santa Pod in July 1973 were awesome to say the least. Incredible ground-shaking beasts that filled the air with the sort of noise you might expect from an erupting volcano. They lost themselves within a thick wall of type smoke as the pair launched simultaneous burnouts from just behind the start line.

The two cars were in fact the American built and raced Stardust Plymouth Barracuda Funny Car campaigned by Don Schumacher and the STP Plymouth Duster bodied car of Paula Murphy.

Don Schumacher above and below his car Stardust

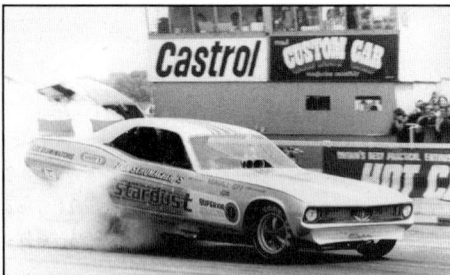

The very top end of drag racing was in Nobby's blood, and had been since his first introduction to the sport in the late 50s, so you can imagine his elation at standing within a mere few feet of what was sheer automotive force beyond his wildest dreams. I knew from the moment we stood together watching them from close to the start line that Nobby would not settle until he had one.

The two cars stayed in the country for a short series of meetings with their respective drivers, who entertained us with two further spectacular shows before handing the cars over to Santa Pod Raceway, who had purchased them to enhance and expand the already growing drag racing facility they were developing in Bedfordshire. During the initial negotiations the owners of the raceway had approached Nobby, knowing he was probably the only contender with the necessary enthusiasm, drive, knowledge and experience to ask if he would be prepared to take on and run the STP car.

Nobby couldn't have asked for more and we, the team, were over the moon at the prospect of having the chance of caring for and commanding such a mighty beast.

The next two Funny Car meetings gave us a much needed opportunity to learn the finer points of what differs between the dragsters we had, over the years become so used to, and the rather different techniques needed to make the seemingly very short wheel base cars perform. I recall the setting of the massive multi-plate slider clutch with the need to disassemble it and re-shim the six main support posts after each run and get the settings exactly right for the track conditions, as being one of the more daunting tasks. Nobby proved able to master this mainly, I think, through his genuine and possibly unique understanding of what really went on in the clutch on a run. Later slider clutches we used incorporated screw adjustment on the posts which allowed for quicker easier adjustment but still gave no clue to where they needed to be set for any particular track or weather condition. This was still down to the team leader, Nobby.

Possibly my biggest shock of all time was the point at which Nobby offered me the chance to drive, or should I say pilot the car.

I donned a freshly tailored-to-fit multi layer Nomex

fire suite, something akin to an old fashioned tea cosy rather than a more flimsy fire proof circuit racing garment, and this on top of full coverage Nomex underwear socks and balaclava. Following this, Simpson fire boots, face mask, with mere tiny holes in front of the eyes (all the best available spec at the time), helmet and gloves. We are all well aware that even the best of fuel engines are prone to failure with the ever present threat of turning into an instant fireball during the run and Nobby was determined to be prepared at all cost.

The engine had been warmed and prepared for the run and was sitting some distance behind the start line with the body raised ready to accept a very willing, though perhaps a little tentative, pilot. I slid into the opening behind the massive engine, somehow straddling the steering column, and lowered myself into the snug fitting seat.

Nobby leaned in beneath the still supported body of the car pulling the two shoulder straps down to meet the central lock for the five part harness. He then tugged the free ends of the straps forward with some force to ensure I was well and truly at one with the super high strength chrome-molybdenum steel roll cage which formed part of the Kent Fuller-Romeo Palamedies chassis of the car.

Controls all came neatly to hand and the seat felt like it was made for me. There was no way to disengage the Crowerglide clutch other than to reduce engine rpm. The left foot pedal was the brake and on the right the loud one. Hand controls included fuel shut-off, magneto kill switch, the two speed transmission shift lever, reverser and parachute release.

NOBBY'S QUARTER MILE

As our turn came the massive 24 volt starter motor was slotted into the front of the engine and Nobby pressed the start button. The giant motor span over eagerly for a few seconds while the oil pump sent the thick 70 weight racing oil surging through the engine and up into the rocker gear on top of the cylinder heads. This done all went very quiet for a moment as the giant butterfly flaps on the front of the air intake were opened and Nobby rapidly injected about half a pint of petrol into the waiting giant chasm of the bug catcher with the aid of a squeeze washing up liquid bottle. The flaps, now released, sprung shut again. The waiting was over. Nobby once again pressed the magic button and the familiar whirr of the engine being spun over signalled me to release the magneto kill switch. Instantly the engine erupted into life.

The unmistakeable cackle of the nitro-burning engine sounded very different from within the car, almost quiet, more of a deep vibration.

I felt very alone, somehow isolated from the outside world and now in total control of what would happen next. I pressed my left foot firmly onto the brake pedal as the starter was quickly unlatched, the body inched up a tad, to allow the prop to be whipped out by one of the crew and then lowered down and firmly locked into place by Nobby himself.

Vision was limited by the face mask and seating arrangement to a relatively narrow band directly through the front windshield of the car which, in itself, seemed a mile in front of me with side vision simply non existent. So I was left to rely entirely on the directions delivered by what had become the legendary figure of our leader. Nobby had acquired an unmistakeable image on the

Santa Pod start line wearing his cowboy boots and Stetson as he orchestrated the Houndog performances, directing the cars and guiding them back to sit squarely on the hot rubber tire tracks laid only seconds earlier. A very vital performance if we were to succeed making the cars perform in those very poor surface conditions compared to Santa Pod today. Being well aware of the need to position the car very directly in line with the direction of the strip I had with Nobby's guidance managed to position it, I thought, well straight.

Nobby walked almost cautiously away from the car heading toward the start line while I kept my left foot on the brakes awaiting instruction while the engine rumbled away quite happily anticipating the moment it would be brought back to life.

The signal was given for the crew to apply a splash of bleach in front of each rear tyre and I gently eased off the brake to allow the two 17 inch wide slick tyres to creep onto the wet patches, reapplied the brakes and pulled the Lenco transmission shift lever back into top gear. Nobby gave the go sign.

As my right foot hit the 'loud pedal' all hell broke loose as the engine erupted into the 2000 horse power beast it really was. I felt myself being lifted as the two huge slicks spinning at over 200 miles an hour on the fine asphalt surface grew as smoke started to pour off them and the car accelerated toward the start line. My vision of the gantry at the far end of the strip moved rapidly to the left of the windshield and out of sight with the Christmas tree now directly in front of me. A shed load of left hand down brought me looking back towards the finish line and I shut off the power before breaking to a stand still. I was able to engage reverse gear by the time Nobby had appeared in front of me and directed me back onto the rather snaky lines of rubber I had left behind. A second burnout proved less dramatic and not as strong as the first one. Following this I was able to stage and on the green light achieve a launch off the line with a premature shut off and coast through to the finish concluding satisfactorily, my initial mandatory part pass to satisfy the authorities.

I had been at an engineering college in Thame when I attended the International Drag Fest at Blackbushe and was enthralled by the engineering aspect of creating vehicles that would accelerate and travel quicker than anything else.

On leaving college in the summer of 1966 I worked with a major construction equipment distributor in Hatfield and was thrilled to meet Nobby there. At the time he was in the process of constructing Houndog 3. I couldn't believe my luck when Nobby accepted my offer to help work on the car. They were happy days with Mike Hutcherson driving the car and he and a strong and very willing team carrying out the unending work needed to keep the cars running. With Mike not working on the premises, there were times when we needed to do engine runs and test launches on the significant lengths of tar mac at the Olding's site in Hatfield. I willingly stepped into the seat to do this. Over the period of time we found ourselves undertaking a fairly heavy development program to overcome mechanical failures and produce more powerful and faster cars leading up to the building of Houndog 6 prior to taking on the Funny Car in 1973.

Racing the Funny Car proved to be something else beyond belief, there were incredible highs, but not always, there were also times when things

Owen Hayward of the Houndog team wins again

went wrong. The feeling during and after the first incredible burnouts is indescribable with winning races and achieving good performances the ultimate. Filling the promenade in Brighton with smoke at the Brighton speed trials and doing spectacular fire burnouts at Santa Pod all added to the excitement and enjoyment.

However all good things must come to an end and my decision to move on came during 1984 when I announced my decision to retire at the end of that season.

Without Nobby's unequalled drive and determination to be at the top in drag racing come what may, coupled with his exceptional talent and engineering skills none of this could have happened.

The proof of this can be witnessed in that despite overwhelming difficulties in the form of an horrific accident and the tragic loss of his daughter Jodie, he has battled on against all odds to complete his latest creation, an entirely new Funny Car scheduled to appear in 2008. What an incredible guy!

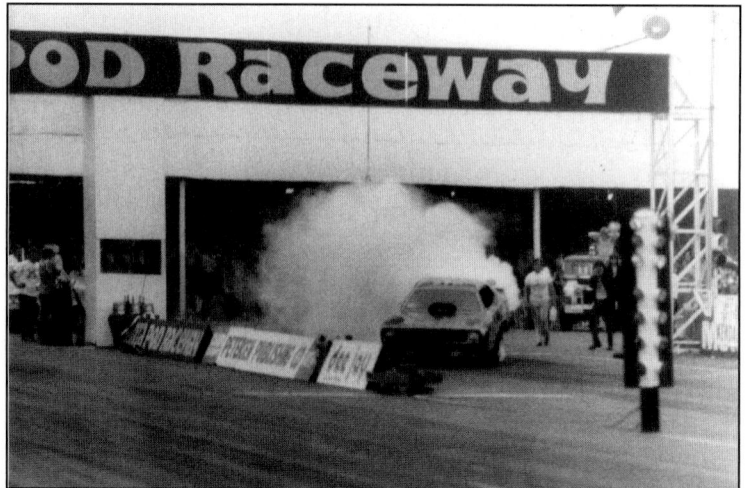

The familiar traffic lights at the famous Santa Pod Raceway

In 1974 ...

You shouldn't believe all you hear!

We were as usual putting on a good show with the Duster and the Fueller. Wherever we went we started to have a good following and a reputation for our smokey burnouts. Things were looking good.

One day at Santa Pod, after we returned to the pits from another qualifying run, a gentleman approached me to say what a show we were putting on and how the crowd appreciated what we were doing. He said, "I think I would be interested in sponsoring this team", with this I smiled, as money was always tight, we were busy but I took time out to speak to him for about fifteen minutes. I could not help but notice how well spoken he was. I said, "once we have cleared the pits up why not come round to the caravan as we are having a barbecue and you are more than welcome?" He enquired if his Rolls Royce would be okay in the field. I said if he wasn't happy he could park it beside our caravan, he said that would be fine. So we made a date, we had one more qualifying run to complete and I left him saying see you around seven. We finished our qualifying run, packed the car away, cleaned up and retreated to the van. The gentleman returned to us just after the agreed time. Showing my hospitality I immediately poured him a large whisky. He explained his position in a large company with which I immediately poured him more whisky. I told him about the costs of a nitro team, he seemed to fully understand the commitment to the costs and the part he could possibly play as a team sponsor. I couldn't have been more excited, the thought of extra finance could only mean faster times for both cars. We exchanged telephone numbers and he said to leave it about a week and give him a call, as he was away on business. The thought of the extra money and involvement of a big sponsor could make me a happy man. The week soon came round I called the numbers on the business card and to my astonishment and disappointment the gentleman turned out to be the managing director's chauffeur, hopefully I learnt something here.

Andy Willsheer
A very good friend from the 70's recollects ...

If I recall correctly, it was in 1972 that I first went along to Santa Pod Raceway. A friend on the building site in Cheshunt where I was working at the time convinced me of the merits of a day at the drags. Trekking along to the rural locale, I was struck by the variety of machinery assembled to assault the quarter-mile strip. And when the fuel cars on hand were fired, it was not only a case of sensory overload but also a rapid realisation that this was a sport I could really get into.

One of the slingshot dragsters at the meeting was called Houndog and the team was led by a tall gentleman wearing a straw hat and flip flops. This was, of course, the man himself, Nobby Hills, orchestrating the mechanical work on the early-model Hemi that motivated the machine. Over the course of ensuing years, my life became increasingly wrapped up in the 1320 world, both in the UK and USA, the latter following an initial visit in late 1973 that extended from a planned stay of three months to a full year and three months.

Nobby's involvement extended from a single dragster to a two-car team with the addition of the Paula 'Miss STP' Murphy Plymouth Duster flopper that was brought across the Pond to race at the Pod by the Phelps' family, and the rest is... as they say ... history.

He and his hired drivers—Movin' Mike Hutcherson, Alan Bates and Owen Hayward are the shoes I remember – always looked the part ... and the team cars invariably performed impressively.

I was pleased to see the new Houndog AA/FC unveiled at the NEC's Autosport International show in January 2004 and look forward to seeing Nobby Hills' moniker gracing a race meeting in the very near future.

Andy Willsheer

Nobby says: Andy Willsheer Photo Journalist in the 70s I remember always gave the Houndog team a very good write up. I eventually met up with him and formed a lasting friendship up until the unveiling of my new car in 2004.

1975 ...

Memories of an average weekend's drag racing for the team

Nobby and his team usually arrive from Ware in Hertfordshire on the Friday evening and stay overnight in their caravan that is kept at the Pod racetrack. They bring one of the cars (the Funny Car usually) and Owen will bring the other, as at this time they were running two cars.

The week prior to the racing most evenings are spent ensuring pistons and parts are all working and any replacements that usually were ordered from the States had arrived.

By the Saturday the first autograph hunters of the day generally approached the team *(yeah we felt quite famous at times)*. They generally took a few snapshots of the team and car.

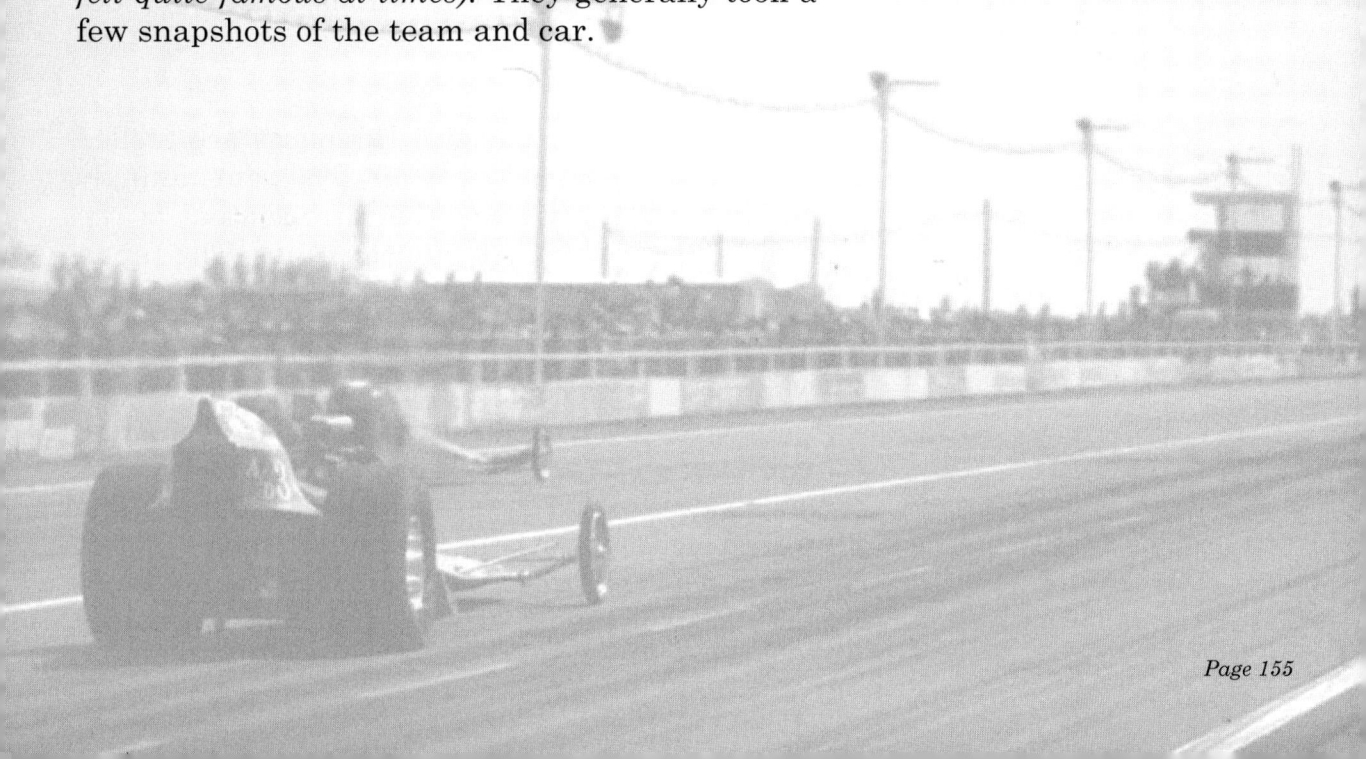

The rest of the morning is also spent shining up the fibreglass shell of the car to ensure it glitters for its special performance. Alan Bates generally kept an eye on the wheel nuts leaving nothing to chance. The team always carried bin loads of spares, cans of oil, plastic carboys full of nitro and enough tools to equip a chain of garages.

Late morning Owen, the driver, usually arrived with the digger dragster along on the trailer. The long rail is gingerly manoeuvred out of its close fitting trailer and immediately it too is polished. The mechanic then fitted the airfoil to the back end and started the preparation for the as yet untested engine's first warm up run.

By midday the scrutineering begins. Its over in a matter of minutes then back to the pits for an oil pressure warm-up on the funny car engine.

Generally down the road other motors are fired up and the show is starting to begin with crowds gathering around to the strong sounds of the engines. Minor adjustments are made and the show is ready to roll.

By quarter to two the two Houndogs are fuelled and ready to run. Nobby always painstakingly checked and re checked the nitro content of the fuel as £90 worth goes into the tanks. The funny car ran on 84 per cent and the digger 90 per cent.

The rear of the funny car was jacked up and Owen wearing a face mask climbed in. Nobby then connected the 24 volt electric starter, Alan was normally on hand with a fire extinguisher, ready for instant use, in case of a blowback. The engine was turned over with the ignition off, then stopped, petrol was then squirted into the butterflies and then POW – the amazing sound that only comes from a big blown engine on a heavy nitro load. The crowds gather as the noise and hot nitro fumes fill the air. The throttle would then be jabbed by Nobby. Owen would check out the clutch and reverser. After its over the silence is deafening.

Three o-clock and the top fuel dragster was pushed into the fire up road ready for an oil pressure run. Usually there was a ten minute or so wait to get to the front of the queue and get a signal to go. The push car would accelerate down the tar mac until with any road left the engine would fire up. Owen was always popular with the crowds at this stage and they cheered him on merrily. This was usually a run with no burnouts just a stately progress down the strip to warm up the motor. Back at the pits then for more preparation on the engine in readiness for the qualifying run later on in the afternoon.

By quarter to five both of the engines of the two cars would be ready for qualifying. Street plugs were used only for warm ups so were changed, valves and ignition set and the clutch of the funny car torqued down to a final setting. Nobby flitted from car to car keeping an overall eye on things but the mechanics were in charge of their own cars.

By 6.30 Owen is suited up and strapped into the claustrophobic recess of his car. The engines fire up beautifully and the lid goes down over him. The team then go into a well rehearsed routine. Alan's with bleach for the burnouts, Nobby always ran up the track guiding Owen back on to his tyre marks and Alec would gun the engine of the push car, ready to race up the strip as soon as the funny car let loose.

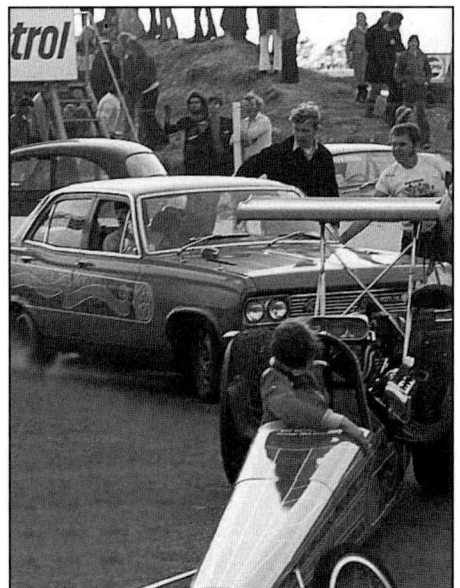

The burnouts left an amazing white cloud of smoke that billowed over the track as Owen inched the straining car into stage. The Christmas tree lights hit green and the engine noise reaches a crescendo and suddenly its all over and the push car's accelerating down the strip towards the parachute billowing in the distance.

The commentators would get excited as would the crowds. Then the funny car would be towed back still with smoke coming from its headers. It always seemed a long road back to the pits. The timeslip was filled in and congratulations were given by the timekeeper.

Back at the pits adjustments are made again. Most of the team members at this time have their well deserved break and snatch some tea. By now it is dark and the lights are on and there is a greenish-white hue over the strip. Owen gets suited up again for the next qualifier. The cars tend to look pretty good under the floodlights.

By 10pm qualifying is over and then its relaxation time and Nobby would be known to stoke up a glowing barbecue between the caravans. Lots to eat, lots to drink and lots of tall stories were told after a hard days racing.

The fire goes down and the lucky ones go to their caravans or hotels to sleep for the night while the rest use tents and sleeping bags. The next day is an eight o-clock start.

8.00am and time to rise. The funny car has been checked, and bearings are altered on the engine. The dragster has its clutch stripped as Nobby felt there was a dished pressure plate and then the valves were also reset.

NOBBY'S QUARTER MILE

All this takes until about 11.00am. By then the pits are packed with onlookers and the prospect of a good capacity crowd for the afternoon. By midday the dragster is put back together and ready for a warm-up and oil pressure run.

The afternoon is similar to the one before filled with burnouts and the funny car and digger go through their paces. This goes on until 9.00 pm when the meeting will come to an end and another exciting weekend end.

Nobby and the team have enjoyed themselves in a sport which puts on a very good show.

Brothers Grimm memorial

1975 ... Shows

In Germany, Sweden and Austria

We often went to different countries with the dragster and on one occasion whilst walking around the town square in Hanou, Germany, we spotted a very impressive statue. On walking over and looking at it we realised it was of the Brothers Grimm the fairy story writers. It is only now that this holds a special memory as later on they became a favourite story book read to my small daughter Jodie.

I have always had a fascination with airships so when we were visiting Germany in Friedrichshafen lakeside on the border of Germany and Switzerland we came across the Zeppelin Museum. This was very fascinating and on seeing what used to happen to the airships when they were being developed I noticed they were inflated with gas on the lake by the factory. One exhibit was the nose cone from the one that had burnt out and crashed in New England in May 1937 (the Hindenburg). Being a gas welder I was surprised to see the aluminium struts were all gas welded by oxy acetylene the same way in which I had been doing to my drag racing cars!

During that time when we were racing, the cars we raced against and very often beat, were Dennis Priddle in his blue Monza, Dave Stone in Stardust and Alan

NOBBY'S QUARTER MILE

Herridge in Gladiator and Alligator.

Also this year we took in two meetings in Sweden. We made many trips to Mantorp Park, Sweden with the Duster Funny Car also with Stardust to match race. On one trip to Stockholm travelling in my car with me was the Joker Ron Picardo. We visited the Funny Girl Nightclub and also a sex shop. Ronnie purchased a strap on thing while we were driving around Stockholm Ronnie strapped this thing on his forehead and proceeded to swing out on the rear door of my car shouting at the top of his voice. Yes Ronnie was always good fun!

In the Alps

Hockenheim stadium – drag strip

1976 ...

A famous face in the drivers seat!

I was asked to go to Crystal Palace where Desmond Lynham, for the sake of a promotional film for Santa Pod, had to appear to drive the Houndog. What great fun this was as it was filmed with Desmond getting in and being strapped down and then getting out of the car. I closed the car down and then opened it up again and let him out. It was the middle bit he did not do, this was left to Owen!

So yes we did the real thing and Owen did his usual burnout which was fantastic. He burnt out the full length of the straight and shut the motor down coming to stop round a left hand bend about 10 yards from a gate across the original old grass track.

30 plus years of friendship

– A former policeman's eye view! ... on Norman 'Nobby' Hills

Nobby and John Pooley

I have known Nobby for over 30 years now and at that time during the 70's I was a motorcycle traffic cop. Many people would say that they were not the most popular guys to meet, especially if one loomed in your rear view mirror, perhaps for travelling too fast. Nobby I think met one of my colleagues under just similar circumstances. I don't think he fell 'foul' of him but I do remember that I was able to 'square' Nobby's transgression! At this time Nobby was working at SLD Oldings, and we *(the police)* used their weighbridge facilities. Nobby would sometimes assist in unloading overweight vehicles and help us in anyway he could.

I found him to be a genuine person and I think he realised that I had an interest in machines that went fast. It was also around this time that I was introduced to the world of 'Houndog' and the building of dragsters, funny cars and trailers. I also became more familiar with such names as Pontiac and Chevrolet, these being much more interesting than Minis or Range Rovers.

I spent many hours watching the building of funny cars and engine builds in the workshops of SLD Oldings. I know that Nobby also spent many hours burning the midnight oil at Oldings. He was there many evenings and often at weekends building, modifying and putting final touches to his cars.

I was intrigued with the welding and meticulous building of a chassis and the expertise that went into its completion. I was also very impressed with, even at that time, the safety issues that were paramount to building a 'safe' dragster or funny car.

I went to Santa Pod and saw the 'team' perform. At this time the guy who drove for Nobby was Owen Hayward. I was amazed at the raw power of these race machines, the noise, smell and adrenaline buzz from all involved. When Nobby was in race mode I saw him in a different light. He was a very imposing tall figure like a Texan landowner with his Stetson, shades and boots but he ran his team with firm authority and with the occasional outburst of anger, usually because things weren't going right, and he knew it could be improved upon. It was then time for me to keep out of the way and play the ignorant guest.

But, hey the results were for all to see and the public loved to see Houndog smoking on the burnouts and then disappearing along the quarter mile at a phenomenal speed with low passes. Having seen this a few times I knew that this guy could really build funny cars.

Transportation of these race cars, because of their dimensions, was difficult and there was very little within the British market that was suitable for the job and Nobby therefore decided to build his own trailers, and in particular one of those that was totally enclosed. He has always been professional and a perfectionist and the trailer had to be the best but stay within the legal minefield of road traffic law. We used to spend sometime pouring through legislation so that the end result was 100% appropriate for the job and legal. I suppose

NOBBY'S QUARTER MILE

I considered myself his traffic law advisor!

I think it was around 1984 that Nobby asked if I would like a trip abroad on his behalf. The task was to convey his funny car, a dragster and drag bike to Holland for a static display at a motor show. I will always remember the day before departure Nobby's Chevy Silverado truck complete with trailer was parked outside my house. The only slight problem was that because of its length it was outside my neighbour's house too! My son, who also came on the trip, was about six at the time and he thought it was great, and it was going to be the adventure of a lifetime for him.

Having driven that vehicle and trailer over to Europe along with a mate of mine with a similar but nevertheless inferior rig I then realised Nobby's engineering skill. It drove superbly on motorways as well as over cobbled streets, the performance, balance, stopping power, handling and braking qualities being top class. How many trailers and caravans do you hear of jack-knifing nowadays? Quite a few I'm afraid. I do remember Nobby telling me not to come back unless I had the motor show appearance fee with me!

There was a period when Nobby Hills racing diminished in the 90's but we still remained friends. To jump forward many years I was devastated to hear of his freak accident whereby he had almost blown himself to bits. He must have been so close to death.

Later the loss of Jodie in 2004 was so tragic that I was completely lost for words and felt helpless. Although I did not know Jodie's sister Katie as well as Anne and Nobby I knew that they would eventually pull through together with their own closeness and courage and personal determination.

My friendship with Nobby cannot be described as being in each others pockets, but we know that if either of us need the help or support of the other it will always be there. It just seems incredible as to where the last 35 years have gone, but I am very happy to be able to contribute a few words about my friend Norman 'Nobby' Hills.

John Pooley MBE

Houndog International Drag Racing Supporter Club

John and Brenda Lees remember ...

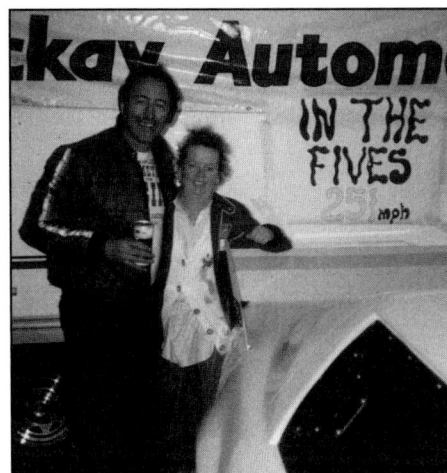

Nobby and Brenda

If anyone had told me that a social evening out would change our lives completely, I would never have believed them, but it happened!

Back in the late 60's and early 70's we went to a local pub nearby to Cuffley in Herts, where we met lots of drivers and owners plus their crews. By the time we left for home John was looking forward to starting a Fan Club for Nobby Hills and his dragster the Houndog.

From then on we were flooded with letters all asking different questions. We sat up late many nights writing back and eventually The Houndog Supporters Club was formed. Nobby and the crew were delighted.

We made lots of friends with everybody and even now as we get older we still keep in touch with many of them.

Running the Club was a pleasure to do and we enjoyed it very much. It was so nice to be part of the popular drag racing team which Nobby Hills put his whole life and soul into. His racing has been greatly admired by all and sundry including many in America and across Europe.

I must have spent a small fortune on sweets over

the years but I never seemed to have any left when we got home. One person in particular had and still has a penchant for chocolate raisins!

As for us, now we are still waiting for one of Nobby's famous chillis!!!

Houndog rules okay – John and Brenda Lees.

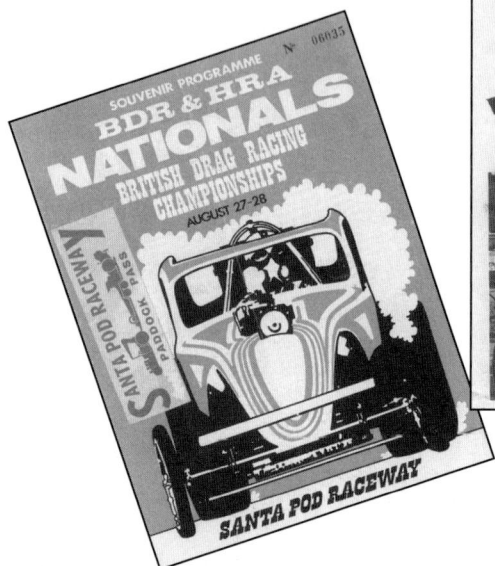

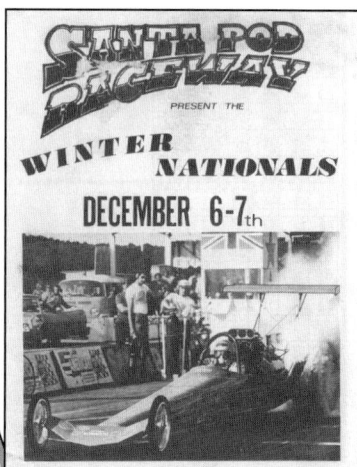

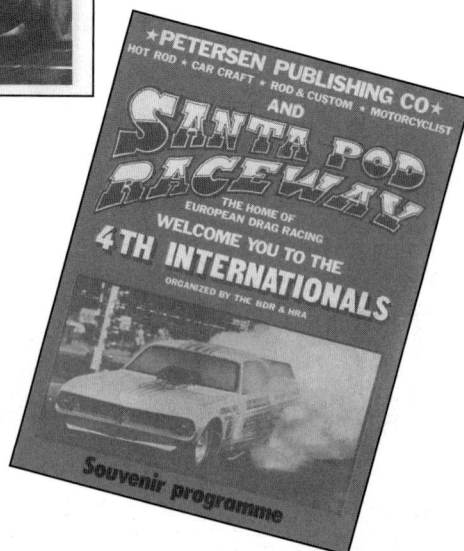

Alan Bates fond, or maybe just memories, of Nobby!

One Houndog driver ...

I could write stories about the things Nobby and I have got up to over the years but we would need a separate book to put it all in, alternatively we could spend a week in a pub, drink it dry and we might just get there!

I first went drag racing in 1969 and started working with Nobby about that time. By 1973 I kept the Duster Funny Car in my mum's garage in Ware and maintained it whilst the dragster

The late Alec Brachtvogel outside Alan Bate's mother's house with Houndog 7 (the Duster Funny Car)

was kept at S.L.D. in Hatfield. At the time I lived with my mum and family in a council house on a quiet peaceful road in Ware, that was until Nobby Hills Racing came along, all of a sudden it was all big Yanks, Burnouts, drag racing up the road and finally one day the ultimate.

We had just finished servicing the Duster and as we were due to go racing the next day we needed to run the car, so after asking my neighbours if it was alright to run the car up and down, we did just that! But they sure are noisy outside our house, the kids came round from miles around so poor old mum suffered again!!

Nobby and I have probably fallen out with each other more than anyone else I've known, but only ever once whilst racing, two years after the death of my old mate Tony Boden in Hockenheim. Nobby was asked to do some observed demo runs at the German track to prove that funny cars could be safe, and as I had been Tony's crew chief up until a year before he died so for me to be the next driver to run they were real tense times. On that particular day Nobby and I were really at each other but eventually he said let's just get this done which we did but that was one day I was glad to get over with.

One time I remember when we were doing burnouts for potential Houndog sponsors we always seemed to hit problems, we managed to put a brick through the windscreen of a Mercedes that belonged to the Managing Director and worst still we smashed a massive plate glass window at General Motors in Belgium.

I have been asked my opinion of Nobby so here goes ... ***Nobby is selfish ... single minded ...***

arrogant and probably lots more besides ... but what you see is what you get, I've known Nobby through the rough and the smooth and it's basically being like this that has got him to where he is today.

Nobby has always worked long hours and will not suffer anyone who does not also. Many people do not like the big hat, the country music and the attitude but that's Nobby and if you don't like it – tough.

I personally think that drag racing has suffered without Nobby, there are no personalities any more and at least he will put the show back into funny cars again. I have learnt so much, some good, some bad, being around Nobby and would like to wish Nobby and the crew all the best and I can't wait for Nobby's next quarter mile.

Nobby Hills: The man, the myth, the legend

by Chris Blows *a former crew member and webmaster to www. houndogdragracing.co.uk and nhracing.com*

I was honoured to be asked to write something about the big man for this book, but didn't know where to start. There are so many old "war stories" of racing days gone by that I am sure will be covered elsewhere in this book, so I don't want to add any of my own. I spent a considerable portion of my late teens and twenties being in and around and working with Nobby and his team and even after I left the team and stopped all interest in the sport (and regrettably lost touch with Nobby), I looked back to those times and the stories with many fond memories.

So what is it about the man that creates such loyalty, respect and affection in those that come into contact with him? I don't want this to sound like a eulogy, but maybe this tale goes some way to explain it....

I set up a website, www.houndogdragracing.co.uk, in early 2001 to chronicle the history of the man and the team and was astonished about the interest it generated. Then news came through that he was considering building a new car. My late wife asked my what I thought..." I don't know, I would have thought hell will freeze over before he builds another one" was one of my responses to her I think ... Oh well, shows what I know !

Moving on a year or so; September 2003, I went back to Santa Pod with my two teenage daughters, one of whom was wearing one of her mother's very old Houndog T Shirts which, for some inexplicable reason, had never been thrown out.

Walking around the pits, I noticed someone looking intently and pointing at my daughter. He nudged the guy standing next to him who then recognised me.

It was Nobby.

It had been 18 years since we had last met but the conversation and jokes flew like it had been 18 days. Both of us had been through some tough times, his being well chronicled in this book. Despite my interest in the new car and all things racing related, he was far more interested in being introduced to my daughters. They had both been brought up on a diet of old drag racing stories and to meet the man that had been central to many of them left an impression on them that has endured to this day. While he obviously wanted to show off the pictures he had of the new car, he was more interested in meeting my children and involved them in the explanation of where the car was in its development and the plans for the future.

Every time we meet or talk, he enquires as to the well being of my girls and more recently when I introduced him to my new partner, always wants to be remembered to her.

In summary, he can deal equally well with princes and paupers and has that ability, that so few people have, in making someone feel important.

He is intensely sociable and approachable. He is amusing and while larger than life in many aspects, he is also somewhat modest in some and continuously surprised at how the interest has been unrelenting in the developments of the new team and car.

While he has incredible engineering and mechanical skills, turning on a computer is a skill that has so far eluded him. His use of a TV remote control has also been known to be questionable.

Did I mention he likes a beer and is partial to Country music ?

Chris Blows

Following on to the late 70s-80s

*B*eing part of the Nobby Hills Drag Racing Team made for all the family a very busy and extremely exciting time. We travelled, raced and enjoyed life meeting many famous faces on the way including attending demos and even doing TV appearances.

It was during these years my personal life changed dramatically, I met Anne in 1973 who later became my wife in 1980, then I became a father for the first time with the birth of my daughter Jodie Lou in 1978, then a second daughter Katie Jo in 1984. Also in 1978 I purchased a mobile home in a trailer park at Hooks Cross near Stevenage and lived there for about four years then after that we were able to get a deposit by selling this to get our first home – a bungalow.

Whilst doing a demo show at Aintree in 1977 I also met up with the great late Roy Castle, he was very interested in the car and a very nice chap.

In 1978 I met up with some of the stars of American Drag Racing, Jim Dunn, Dick Lahaie, Roland Leong, Harvey Crane, Keith Black, Shirl Greer, Larry and Tony Miglizzy (L&T Clutches) and of course the lovely Linda Vaughan Miss Hurst. I had my photograph taken with her and Keith Black at the Sema Show in Las Vegas. I also met Eddie and Ercia Hill, Tom "Mongoose" McCewan, Shirley Muldowney at Pomona was kind enough to sign pictures for Jodie and Katie.

Above: Shirl Greer and below Nobby, Jodie and Shirley Muldowney

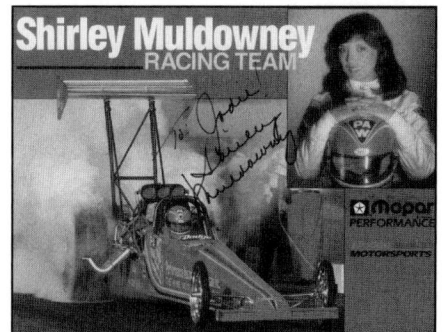

Meeting Big Daddy

Don Garlits

During 1976 I worked with Big Daddy (Don Garlits) when he came over. I was very lucky I had a spare 426 engine and at the time he was short of parts. I think some of the shipment went missing, anyway it was a fantastic experience watching and working with the No. 1. He came looking for me at the end of the meets and thanked me shaking my hand.

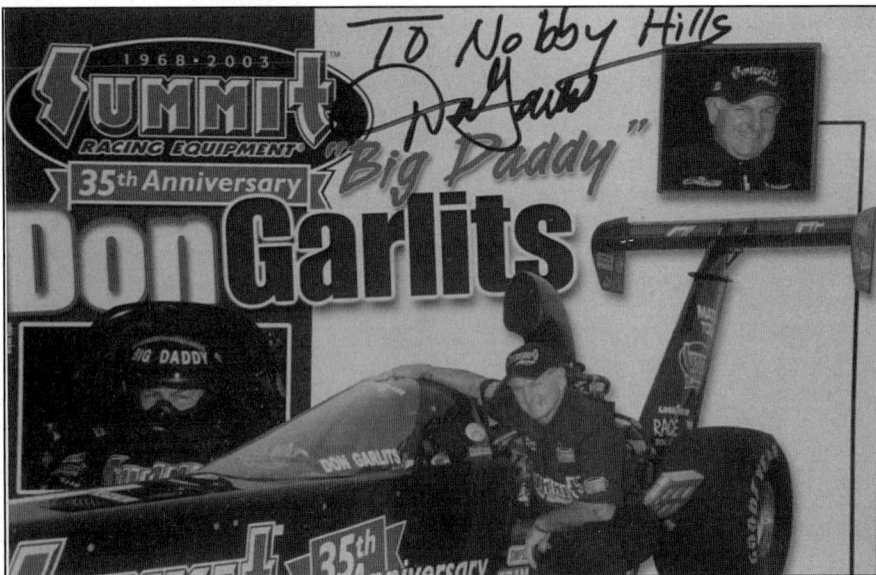

1977 ...

The Duster crashes
Owen writes it off

It was a very sad day on the August Bank Holiday of 1977 when Owen and the Duster parted company, after a hard launch the half shaft sheared in the rear axle. Owen left the line on the pit lane side of the strip as the rear axle let go the car took a violent swerve to the right at the spectator fencing. The impact rolled the car at least three times coming to a stop right side up three quarters of the way up the strip in the opposite lane he started his journey. When we arrived at the wreck Owen was unconscious and was taken to the local hospital where he stayed in for observation. I was only pleased Owen survived such a hard crash as for the car we could all see that this fabulous Duster was now history.

Dramatic shots of how it all happened!

Left how it ended up

1978 ...

Here are some excerpts of Going for Bust, an article written in Custom Car in 1978 about the progress of the team and the Houndogs ....

Nobby Hills is to Houndog cars what Isaac Newton is to Newton's third law of gravity: i.e. the latter could hardly exist without the former. Or something. He builds the cars, nurses them to perfection, sets them up to run hard and fast and puts them back together again when they go wrong. Sure, he's got one of the best teams in the business behind him, and driver Owen Hayward isn't known as 'The Natural' for nothing but to all Nobby is Houndog racing.

In all he's run nine cars over the years and the team's progress has in many ways echoed the development of dragging in this country. Rung one of the ladder, the first Houndog of all hit the limelight at the 1965 International Drag Festival. During the previous year an all star American touring team had come over to show us just what drag racing was all about, and the upshoot was a whole fleet of British built rails and altereds. Drag racing suddenly became a real live sport rather than something you saw in Frankie Avalon movies or on the pages of Hot Rod. Nobby was quick off the mark with a slingshot dragster powered by a blown carburetted Jaguar engine which used believe it or not lorry tyres on the back, because slicks were hard to come by and ultra expensive in those early days.

Six rails and one funny car later the next car is to be the Houndog 9 which was to be an ultra modern state of the art flopper. Fate took its hand when the Houndog 7 was totalled in an horrific accident at the 1977 SPR August Bank Holiday Meet. In a match race against Roz Prior, a half shaft – supposedly indestructible according to its American manufacturers sheared in two just off the line. In a funny car under full power this has just about the same effect as going into an instant 90 degree turn and that's bad news when you're running 17 inch slicks and a locked differential. Despite prodigious efforts on Owen's part the car went completely out of control, broadsided into the safety barrier and rolled end over end before coming to rest; a twisted heap of jagged metal and cracked glass fibre. Owen was pulled out of the wreckage unconscious, but essentially unhurt but with a major headache.

With construction of the new car already under way, the crash wasn't too much of a blow to the team.

1978 ...

Chevy Pup Houndog 9 Vega (built over the winter of 1977, launched March 1978)

I started drawing up plans for a new funny car in 1977 and at this time I quite liked the Chevy Vega lines so Roy and Bob decided to mould me a body off of their Vega. I persuaded them to graft on an extra pair of headlights, this I felt would make it a little individual and it was. When I collected the body from FGR I took it to SLDO works where I had more thoughts on the body lines. I took a saw to it and cut a wedge out of the top starting at the front being six inches wide back to the spoiler.

The only piece that was not cut was the rear body upright. So we were able to close the front and glass it together. This was done and the body was painted before the Duster was written off. We were lucky enough to have a new funny car back on the strip within a short period of time. We used the engine from the Duster and Bob and Roy supplied me with a brand new Lenco Ford Funny Car rear end. This was a great car from day one a 'Chevy Pup'.

SPR Spring Bank Holiday 27-29th May 1978 there was a little bit of dampness around so I was able to do something a little bit different to help entertain the crowds. With the help of DLT and the directors of SLDO we put the 'Pup' in the back of a 30 ton dumper truck (pay load that is) at the top end of the strip and DLT drove this monster down to the start line area. On stand-by was a 50 ton telescopic crane (owned by SLDO) which we then proceeded to strap to the car and lift it up. The crowd were well pleased and the SLDO directors were pleased with the publicity of their equipment.

Later as the weather improved Owen got the Pup up into the 6s for the first time, 6.93 at this meeting. DLT also did some observed runs in my ex Houndog 8 dragster, which reappeared with its new FGR body, radio one stickers and a black paint job, eventually this job was renamed the Needle. His first full run on 7.37 and he also won this meeting with a 7.53 at 171mph. Dennis Priddle ran best FC time of the meet 6.7 at 207mph.

FATHERHOOD

Later on in August of this year I became a proud father for the first time to my lovely daughter Jodie Lou.

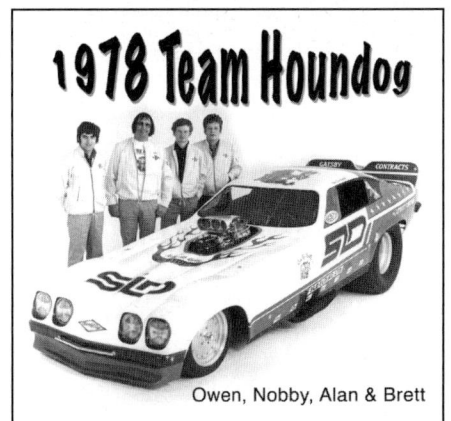

1978 Team Houndog

Owen, Nobby, Alan & Brett

1979 ... Meetings to remember

Santa Pod Summer Internationals & Supernationals, Sugarbeet County and Fireworks meet – race reports ....

*I*t was the Summer of 1979 at the Summer Internationals and the return of Sammy Miller who collected the £5000 prize for Europe's first 300mph terminal speed. After a 4.68/245 shakedown run and a 4.43/265 when he inadvertently hit the chutes after a bumpy top end ride, he ran 4.20 seconds with a terminal speed of 307.6mph. To make sure of securing the prize Sammy continued accelerating through the speed traps and ripped the chute to bits. His final run of the weekend was then cancelled.

In Funny Car Raymond Beadle's Blue Max was No.1 qualifier with a 6.57 followed by Gene Snow with 6.75, Alan Herridge's Gladiator with 6.76, Dennis Priddle's Monza with 6.92, Owen Hayward in the Houndog 9 (which was often referred to as the 'Pup' because of the many alterations Nobby made to the Vega body shell making it smaller than other Vega's running at the time) gave us a 6.95 and Ronnie Picardo in The Force with 7.97. In the first round Beadle had a bye and ran the 6.56. Snow was also on a bye and put in a half pass. Herridge went on to beat Owen Hayward with a 6.68/210 to a 7.07. Priddle ran 6.84/196 to beat Picardo who got out of shape and crossed the centre line. In the series Snow beat Priddle with a 6.51 to a 6.75 while Beadle beat Herridge with a 6.34 to a 6.74.

The following meeting at Santa Pod Raceway, Bank Holiday Supernationals August 25/26/27 produced some exciting times. Alan Herridge who survived a fireball run in the Gladiator during qualifying, flipped the Vega in spectacular fashion on the money run against Owen Hayward in the Houndog.

Qualifying saw Owen as a top qualifier in Houndog with a fine 6.50/200mph. Alan meantime went through the traps in a ball of fire on a 6.61/207 pass – burning the chute off and one of the slicks as a result of an oil leak catching light. But Bootsie was back for the elims, even though there was very

Chevy Pup warms the night sky

little paint left on the fibreglass body!

For the final, Gladiator sounded so mean it was unreal. As the Milodon powered Vega left the line, it beaded skywards before getting out of shape and hitting the barrier – the car ending up on its roof. Hayward motored to a 7.38/139 win as Bootsie crawled out and walked back to the start line to a big round of applause from the crowd.

Also earlier on in the year the car appeared June 23rd/24th:

BDR&HRA, in association with Santa Pod Raceway, organised the first Eastern Nationals at the re-named Sugarbeet County Raceway, part of the Snetterton Circuit. The meeting was alleged to have an all time British Drag Racing single-event sponsorship figure of £3000. The entry list included Owen Hayward in his SLD Olding sponsored Houndog 9.

11th-12th August 1979 – Sugarbeet County Raceway – Two funny cars were present, Ronnie Picardo's The Force and Owen Hayward in the Houndog. The only run on the Saturday saw Ronnie with problems, recording a 7.58/179 to Owen's 7.36/154. Owen also put in two further runs on the Sunday in the Houndog at 7.17/200.4 and 7.02/193.4.

SPR Winternationals October 13th and 14th 1979 with a very wet and windy weekend. This meeting saw the last of Nobby Hills and Owen Hayward's Houndog 9 Vega funny car. It was purchased by Dave Prior. Owen ran a couple of match races with Ronnie Picardo in the Force funny car. Ronnie took the first after Owen crossed the centre line near the start. Owen won the second after Ronnie shut off early. Alan Herridge ran the best time of the meet with a 6.34/208 in the Alligator (dragster).

Nobby comments: A best effort for the pup which was 6.46 at 221mph and by this time I had seen the next body I wanted for the Houndog which was a Dodge Challenger and this was going to be the **Houndog 10.**

*Chevy Pup on one of
its European vacations*

Owen burns out at the Pod

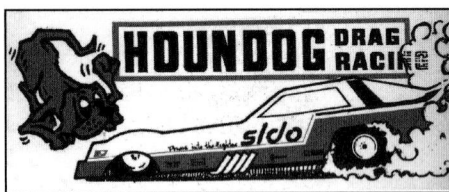

Houndog 10 debut

I built a new chassis for the Challenger with a chromed roll cage. The rest of the chassis was black painted which looked pretty good. This was being constructed whilst we were racing every other weekend.

This car was first seen at the November 1979 Fireworks Meet at Santa Pod.

See race report: Sammy Miller flipped the Vanishing Point rocket car at over 200mph in the dark. The car lifted off the track at the top end after recording a 234mph terminal speed. A cross wind was blamed for the accident as the car took off after passing the end of the spectator banking which, as both racers and spectators know, is a very effective wind break. The extremely light weight of the car did not help matters. Also at this meeting Nobby Hills and Owen Hayward debuted their new Houndog 10 Challenger bodied Funny Car.

Exciting times ahead

I campaigned this funny car for the next three years. We were in the lucky position at that time to have two complete motors one aluminium, Keith Black, and one iron block. I used each one when I felt fit, depending on the need to win at each meeting and of course how the money was.

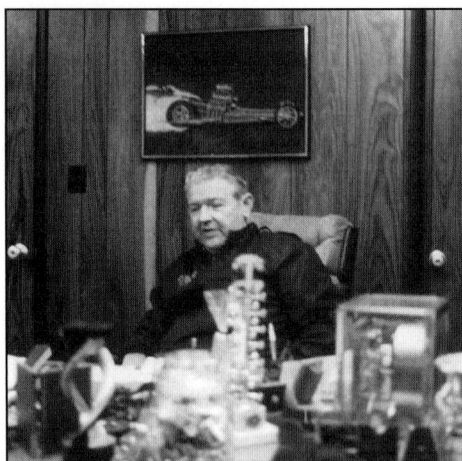

Keith Black

1979 ... Engine Build

At Keith Black USA

I was very lucky to go to Keith Black's in California USA in 1979 and assemble a complete Elephant Motor with a 14.71 blower, everything off the shelves and brand new.

What an experience, Anne was helping me with the parts list, this took me about 3 days. I noticed there was one person in the shop that was showing a lot of interest in what I was up to. In the afternoon of the final day he came up to me and said, "is there something wrong with this engine?" I said, "no way, it's great". He then explained that he had inspected this in total before I had arrived and everything was okay and race ready, parts that is. When I told him how many thousands of miles I would be going from them when it was flown to the UK and that I could not go to a local autoparts and get a KB nut and bolt if one were missing, he then understood my intensity for double checking everything and said I had worried him all week because of this.

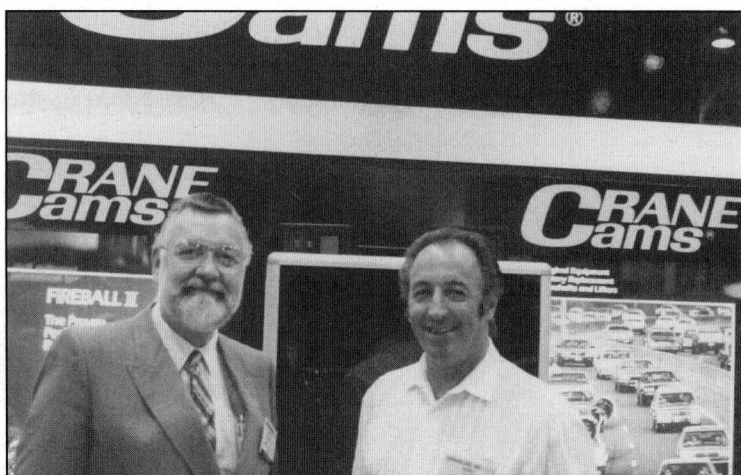

Meeting Harvey Crane

NOBBY'S QUARTER MILE

Also whilst there I walked down a corridor and there were two guys busy sitting on the floor with their legs across the floor. I could not believe my eyes it was Roland Leon and Dick Lahaie, we had a long chat and I felt honoured.

Also in the same complex Fireman Jim Dunn kept his funny car. I made a point of getting to know him and asked him many questions. He was at the time stripping and rebuilding his engine and clutch for the next meet. Every hour or so he would call me over and show me what he was replacing. I'll never forget this and my whole experience over there was very exciting.

With Linda Vaughan (Miss Hurst) and Keith Black

Happy times

Anne's Mum and Dad with another cake!

1980 ... Anne and me
Getting married

Life was always very busy with the cars, and a family as well so by the end of this year Anne and I decided to get married. The date to be exact was 27th December 1980. We decided to keep this on the back burner until about seven days before. This worked out okay really and we had a family reception at Anne's parents house.

Two things occurred, one being that Anne's mum was worried that we did not have a nice wedding cake (as mother's do), so she decided to modify her lovely Christmas cake into our wedding cake. This she did and what a lovely job she made of it – thank you mam.

The other moment was when I in my wisdom opened a large bottle of champagne, not giving a second thought to the recently fitted suspended ceiling. I vigorously shook the bottle and of course the cork went into the lovely ceiling! But we did have a lovely day and it's an easy date to remember my anniversary.

Driving the rig

Anne has always been a great back up to me and a very good co driver for when we travelled for which I have to say well done. On one of these occasions (we had not long been married) we were returning from Germany where we had had terrible cold weather. I remember ice about four inches thick on the side view mirrors on the truck, we had done about five hundred miles with the rig and I decided I needed a rest, so Anne took over the driving, we had about one hundred miles to Calais and I soon fell asleep.

The next thing I knew was the truck coming to a halt and I was absolutely freezing. Both the cab windows were open, I said "what the hell are you doing, I am frozen" Anne replied you may be cold but I have been in a hot sweat driving this sixty foot rig into the docks!" I don't know what else I said but I knew at the time she had done extremely well driving through the Calais traffic at 8 o'clock in the morning – well done honey.

Anne and the family with the rig

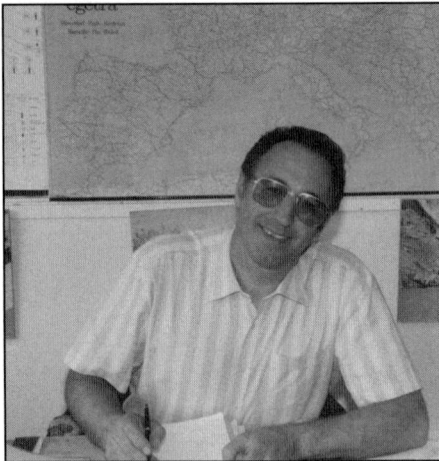

Nobby behind the desk.

My working life progress

at Jack Oldings then SLDO of Hatfield and – self employment

I applied for a job at Jack Olding in 1959 and was paid a fantastic hourly rate of six shillings per hour (30p)! My previous job had only paid three shillings per hour (17p) so this was really good. I loved this job with its interesting fabrication work was just what I needed. I was assembling and welding various things for the construction industry, very large sand driers and buckets of all shapes and sizes, mostly American by design. It was very interesting work and long hours which I wanted. I was able at this time to purchase my second car, a 1951 Ford Consul this was £500 and I had to buy it on HP over three years. After about four years at this job I had worked up to a charge hand in the welding section where there were about twenty five welders in total which made life interesting sometimes and sometimes a little hard. The company generally manufactured and were agents for machines like Vickers, Barber Greene, Hendrix, Rolls Royce oil engines and others.

During the next three years or so I progressed to works supervisor and I had a white coat for this job which also involved the engine and hydraulics side of the business. During this time the largest drag line bucket I was responsible for was a 33 cu yard monster, the weight of this was 27 tons without the dressing, that is chains, spreader bar pin and teeth. When I think back I was responsible for the assembly, this unit had a manganese lip which was 8 inches thick and was welded to the bucket which was one and a half inches thick with a five inch fillet weld on the underside, this was again welded with electric arc with five sixteenths diameter electrodes in stainless, making it some weld!

At that time another job for us was once or twice a year we used to build at the Docks in Southampton – Michigan 475 tractor shovels. They were mostly used on opencast coal sites and the electricity board power stations, they weighed about seventy tons with 12 cu yd and 25 cu yard buckets which I used to design and build at Hatfield. I was also responsible for a 200ft+ long boom for a Lima crane, this was made in seven sections of $8ft^2$, with two 50ft sections and three 20ft sections. These sections were bolted at each joint with sixteen 2 inch machine bolts. This was assembled in the

A very large tyre! (Check out the size of the man beside it!)

Olding yard at Hatfield and then inspected by the insurance company. I dealt with the insurance man on the day of the inspection and took him to the boom and left him to it. Some three hours later I was getting a little concerned because I had not heard from him, so I went to investigate if everything was going well and he showed me what he was doing. He had piano wire tensioned between the centre of the base of the top sections all 200ft. I think he had about 50 kilos of tension and he was checking the straightness with a very large set of micrometers. I asked the obvious question, "what is it like for straight and what was the allowable out of straight?" "Over 200ft" he said, "well this is why I have been out here so long, I cannot find any more than five sixteenth of an inch over 200ft!" He also added that I was allowed two and a half inches, I said great as it was lunchtime now I took him out for a pleasant lunch.

Soon after this I was offered the job of Works Manager. At this time Owen was Service Manager. I suppose this worked very well for us as employees and drag racers.

During this time I was booked to attend a show for construction equipment at Hillhead Quarry. My Director Terry Benn was able to book one of the Hansen Trust's helicopters (our parent company) for the trip. We finally got off the ground at about 1.30pm, the pilot was a young retired naval pilot, a very interesting person to fly with, he explained everything in detail to us whilst we were in flight. We landed at Hillhead quarry on the helicopter landing site. This was to my astonishment in the region of 20 yards to the side of the quarry. We disembarked and made our way to the show stand.

Another fabrication job

NOBBY'S QUARTER MILE

We soon circulated and went to other stands of our competitors and customers. Obviously there was a few beverages at each stand we visited. So by 2.30pm we were quite merry, more stands and a few more beverages I think Terry informed us that we had to assemble back at the helicopter at the latest for a 3.00pm take off.

Opencast coal mine

The quarry

We duly arrived back in time only to see Terry arrive with one of our customers who wanted to fly back to Hatfield with us, he was most impressed that he would be flying back. The pilot did look quite concerned at the extra load so in a businesslike manner he seated us in the correct positions. We were still very merry and quite loud thinking we were kings of the air, the pilot mentioned there might be a problem with the extra passenger, and informed us also that he had completely refuelled and suggest we try to take off. We were rather unaware or perhaps didn't care about the pilot's thoughts, he said, "well gentlemen as we are all strapped in we'll try and give it a go". With quite a roar we felt the motion of the helicopter trying to become airborne, I was suddenly becoming slightly more focused this didn't quite feel right to me as

A gigantic tipper truck sold by SLDO and a man behind it to show size!

we bounced on the skids from left to right, as the helicopter bounced again with quite a thud we suddenly moved and with a shout from the pilot of "tally ho boys" the helicopter made a sudden lurch over the quarry cliff face at that moment we all thought this is it, this is where we are going to end it all, we quickly sobered up only to see our young naval pilot laughing with a pull of the joystick we reared up out of the quarry with an uneventful flight home and a happy landing at Hatfield.

By 1982 I was made responsible for the service exchange and by 1984 Owen left the company. In 1985 I was then promoted again to Works Service and Product Support Manager and Volvo and Michigan merged to form V.M.E. and then I was made redundant. Fortunately I had taken out a redundancy insurance which paid me well for about twelve months.

I then became self employed and I was used mostly by Allied Construction at Billericay as a Management Consultant and Equipment Repairer. This was one of the most rewarding times of my life thanks to the M.D. of Allied Mr. David Jolly. I did this up until 1998 when working for someone and had an industrial accident. This is mentioned further on.

1980 ...

Flying Concorde

I was lucky enough on one of my business trips this year to fly Concorde. New York to Heathrow in just three hours and 20 minutes. I left my hotel in New York 8.00 am and arrived home in Biggleswade at 7 o'clock in the evening of the same day. I found this an awesome experience, it was a lot about what I like, acceleration. Once ready at the start of the runway when we started the acceleration was very good, we seemed to reach lift off speed very quickly and the angle of the seats at this time was new to me, I thought my legs were horizontal to the ground. We then took to the air and you could hear and see the power. After a few minutes the Captain said that we would go out ten miles before we would go supersonic. By this time we would reach about 55,000 ft, the Captain then announced we would go to Mac 1 this we did soon after this he announced we would be going Mac 2, this was incredible, by this time the seat belts were off. A gentleman sitting across the isle to me said "what you need to do now is to walk as

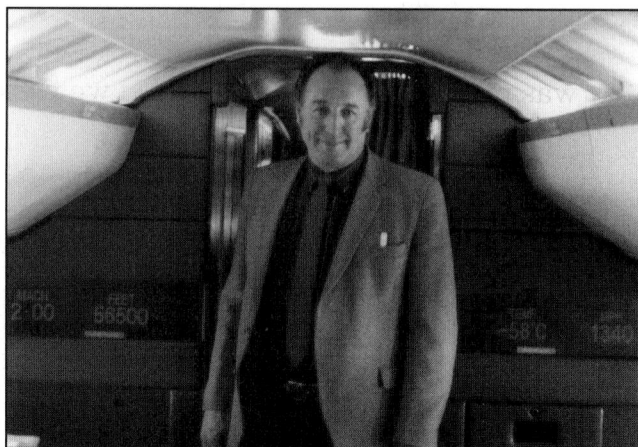

Nobby standing up in Concorde

far down to the tail as possible, then turn round and walk back". This I did, it felt a little bit like walking down hill, going to the tail but when I turned around and tried to walk back this was really different. I needed to lean about 30 degrees towards the front of the aircraft to make the trip back to my seat by this time the read out of air speed was 1250 mph. The gent whose name was Larry said "how about that then?" I did not know what to say I just could not believe it, I said "you did not go and do it", he explained that he'd used Concorde at least once a month for business trips.

After I'd been sitting for about half an hour, Larry said "go and touch the ally hinges on the aircraft door". This I did and guess what, they were hot, the heat had transferred from atmospheric friction outside.

After sitting back down I was asked if I would like to go to the flight deck. I said "yes please" and then I was taken up to a very little room, I was so excited and bewildered that it was difficult to ask any sensible questions. I was there for a few minutes and looked at the screens, then the Captain said, "did you see that?" I said "what was that?" He said "we just passed a 747, stay there and I'll point out the next one". This he did, I tell you I've overtaken some things in my time but nothing like this the 747 was probably doing 600 ++ and we were doing 1300 ++, of course we were 25,000 feet above it. I believe the length of Concorde grows about 10 inches, consequently the inner cabin carpets are overlapped to allow for this. Even coming in to land was awesome, I thought my knees were above my shoulders! Yes my trip on Concorde was very memorable and special now since it has been retired.

1981 ... America

Ronald Regan President of USA

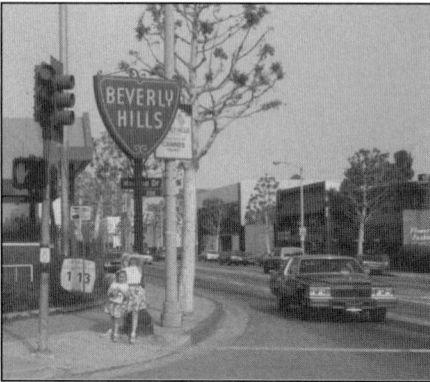

While I was in LA on a trip servicing parts for my race cars I stayed for four nights in the Beverly Hilton Hotel with Anne and the family. Here there was valet parking which I guess was rather strange to us. So I drove the car into the reception area and I stopped the car and immediately a valet appeared, opened the car door, I handed him the car keys, the bellboy was already putting our baggage on to his cart and confirmed our arrival and proceeded to our room depositing

Happy times

our baggage. I tipped him and off he went. We did the usual and then went to the restaurant.

On the second day we decided to have a drive around it was mid afternoon time when I approached the parking valet for my car, he said "I am sorry Mr. Hills, could you please wait for about fifteen minutes the President is about to arrive here. I nearly said "tell me another", but I didn't, after a few moments we went back to our room, I could hear at least two helicopters flying around close by and I think there were four or five gunmen around the entrance. Anyway we left and had our drive around.

The following day we had decided to leave and drive to Vegas. Typically with kids around we were trying to pack our bags and get out in good time, mid morning. In my wisdom I placed our two suitcases just outside the room in the corridor. In around about two minutes there was a very loud banging on the door. I went and opened it and lo and behold there were two men standing there with machine guns at the ready. They asked me if the suitcases were mine and I told them they were so they told me to immediately take them back into the room explaining that they were concerned about the contents possibly containing explosives. I immediately obeyed, as one would with machine guns around! We decided to wait awhile before we left but did eventually get away.

I found out later that it was not a joke and apparently the President at the time, Ronald Regan, had been in attendance at the hotel and they had felt our bags were a threat. It was the nearest I had ever come being near to a President and added to my experiences of travelling in the USA.

Notice that amused Nobby seen in a shop on Route 66 in USA

John Price – 'Captain Chaos'

Commentator and Sky Sports presenter

NOBBY QUOTE: *"I remember way back meeting Captain Chaos who was, would you believe, at the time on roller skates and I think from then on his eagerness to understand the sport made us talk and talk and we have not stopped since!"*

Here John Price gives us his opinions and memories on his friendship with Nobby.

John Price interviewing Jodie Hills shown on men and motors – like daughter like father! because of her love of cars and drag racing. It featured Jodie and her Pontiac car

NOBBY'S QUARTER MILE

The dictionary definition of "houndog" – used in hunting, to pursue, to harass, to urge, to incite.

I couldn't imagine better words to sum up the man behind the drag racing Houndog Nobby Hills.

When I arrived on the scene at the start of 1981, never having attended a drag racing event in my life, Nobby Hills and his team were already acknowledged as one of the front runners in the sport. Operating in the highest class, i.e. Top Fuel, along with such other notables as Roy Phelps, Dennis Priddle, The Stones, Bootsie, Ronnie the Joker, The Pages', Clive Skilton all of whom are now regarded as "the founding fathers". At this point, bear in mind, that racing at the Pod was only some fifteen years old, Brian Taylor, the existing commentator had hung up his microphone, and lots of people were already saying that the glory days had been and gone and that the sport was now in gentle decline.

The Houndog Team had a massive fan base and, as was always the case, those fans knew that when the man came out onto the line with his Stetson, flip-flops, usually sun glasses and sometimes gaily (if I can use that word) coloured or patterned trousers, then they knew that Nobby had arrived and the show would start and there would certainly be no mention of a decline in effort and presentation.

Now if you can imagine, a commentator trying to talk about a subject he knew nothing about, and in fact before the advent of the web, etc., unable to find the time to bone-up on the subject, due to commitments as a working DJ, then you would think that people such as Nobby would give me a wide berth and hope I would be replaced by someone who at least didn't start the day off with – "well! here's a blue car in the left hand lane and a maroon and white car in the right hand lane" continually calling the track, "a circuit" and generally not understanding the difference between the various classes.

This I can assure you was not the case, as I always found the drivers and riders of course, wanted to help me to learn and understand what I was watching.

Nobby was always one person who would take the time to explain the intricacies of the sport and what he and the team were trying to accomplish and he and I struck up a friendship at that time, which I have to say has not diminished over the intervening years.

Whether this is because we have both suffered the loss of a daughter in our lifetime or whether it is because I always appreciate a team that puts on a great show, I'm not certain; all I know, is the sport will always need a Nobby Hills, i.e. showman, professional, innovative, reliable and with the ability to sink a few when the time calls for it.

Well now, here we are forty years plus down the road at the Pod, the racing, (in my rather humble opinion) is fantastic across all classes thanks to the management team in there, and what is being threatened? the return of Nobby Hills Racing. Already, this has incited a few people – some are aware that if the plans for the new "funny car" come to fruition (what is it now Houndog 14?) then they will be pursued, harassed and hunted down – Nobby will want that Number 1 plate back!

BLOODY GOOD LUCK TO HIM and I hope I'm there to talk about it!   *John Price*

1982 ...

TV appearance: Pebble Mill Challenger Houndog 10

I was asked to go to Pebble Mill with the Funny Car. We did the interview and then the producer asked us to run the funny car up the street outside. He had arranged for the police to shut down the roads so it was okay for us to proceed.

I sat Owen in and fired the engine for the warm up, as we did this I noticed two or three people running over from the studios. By this time the engine was warm enough so I shut it down. It appeared that the noise had stopped two recordings, so I explained to the producer that this was nothing compared to a burnout which he wanted. But he still told us to carry on, so I suggested perhaps we best have a time window of about fifteen minutes and ideally this would be in an hour's time. "No problem, carry on" he said.

So in the next forty five minutes Owen got suited up and I filled the tanks with 98% nitro, well if its going to be good – let's help it! I told the producer that Owen would do a sixty yard burnout and the rear wheels/tyres would be going about 200 mph from a standstill. He said "great!" So we put the funny car in the centre of the street and then the cameras were put in position, there were three cameras which was okay, but one cameraman insisted on positioning his camera about eight yards up the street

no more than six feet from the line of the burnout. I explained to him he might find it better to move a little more to the side, he said "it's okay, I have shot this close to cars before and the producer has given me the go ahead".

So I fired up the car and Alan drove off to the far end of the road with the support truck ready for the tow back. I gave Owen the thumbs up as normal, then I walked up about five yards past the pedestal camera in the road, I signalled Owen to start the burnout which he did in the best Hayward style. Burnouts are good wherever they take place, but on the street they are even better.

The street there was about thirty yards wide and there was no wind, it was impossible to see across the street. I heard the engine shut down so as the smoke cleared I saw the pedestal camera turning slowly round and round, the cameraman was nowhere to be seen. Well I'm blowed, about ten seconds or so later, the continuity girl came running over to me and said "was anyone seriously hurt?" She just could not understand why I laughed, I told her everything was normal. I never did see the cameraman again. This footage was used for the next eight weeks at every showing of Pebble Mill at One.

August 1982 The Cannonball Run

Hayward fastest over the mile

This was a great time for the Houndog team and in yet another unaccustomed burst of heat and sunshine Owen powered the Houndog to victory in the Cannonball Run. His place in the final was not easily won and a mere 0.2 of a second separated him from Alan Herridge after three rounds. The climax was when the Houndog streaked a 200mph quarter to emerge triumphant. Another win for the Houndog and congratulations to Owen.

Nobby and Owen

Later in 1982

Death of the Houndog 10 (burned to the ground)

This car unfortunately burned to the ground at Mantorp Park in Sweden. The Challenger's best run was 234mph with an ET of 6.6 secs. Although this was a very sad occasion as the Challenger has been a true friend to Owen and myself, we did for once make the Swedish TV with the funny car fire and if I recall correctly the front page of one of the Swedish national newspapers. A bit of a blow but I had already mentally told myself that we needed to move on and had already fallen in love with the new Corvette (84 body). After inspecting the remains of the old Houndog 10 I realised a new body was desperately needed, the fire on the Challenger body was so intense that the

body had buckled beyond easy repair. At the time we were very well funded by my employers SLDO. So with a quick phone call to Derek Lawson SLDO at Hatfield I explained my problem. Fortunately for us my next phone call was to order the new Corvette body. I think that's the best phone call I ever made from Sweden. I managed to contact Ken Veney to purchase the body from Odyssey Cars in California, this was to be the only 1984 Corvette Body running nitro funny car in Europe.

Houndog 11 construction

By the time the new body arrived at Oldings in September 1983 I had already constructed a new chassis from the motor mounts forward this was to include the new fuel tank and moving the position of the front wheels to enable me to fit the new body in a very limited time. There were so many alterations to make the Corvette fit. This car was rolled out of its trailer almost a year later at the 1983 Fireworks Meeting.

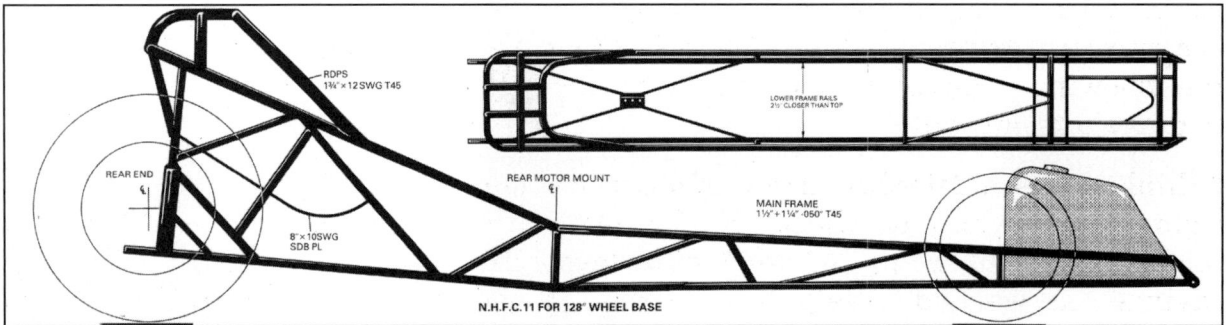

1983 ...

Demag altered avoids the rain! (Houndog 10.5)

During my time at SLDO they often held Company Management Meetings which all the six depots would attend. I was asked by the MD Michael Weeks if we would do a little demonstration with the fuel altered Demag (the Keith Black Hemi). I agreed it was alright as the car was already prepared for a show in Germany the following week. So we cleared the yard ready to do a short burnout.

I think it was a Tuesday, if my mind serves me right. Guess what, it rained. So I spoke with Michael and said "no probs", (one of my favourite sayings), as we had a very large workshop we would do some jumping and hopping inside in the dry.

Okay so we were both properly dressed in our

shirts, ties, etc. and with about thirty directors and managers who stood around watching I strapped Owen into the car. I then fired up the motor, Owen did about three hops forward, great so I backed him up and proceeded to do the same again however on the second hop, the car lurched forward and went by me at 10 mph. Owen cut the fuel which increased the rpm and by now Owen was getting very close to the doors. These were double doors about twenty feet square. Bang, the car then hit one door and passed through the inner liner. Oh dear, I had to get the twenty five ton overhead crane to lift the car back into the workshop.

What had happened was as the car was inside

with the doors were closed, Owen quite rightly
was hopping the car with a lot of brake applied.
On the last hop the disc had removed one of the
callipers from the axle, so no brakes! It took us
about one hundred hours to make a new front end,
repair and get the car ready for its German trip!

I suppose the only good thing about the incident was it did not get wet!

NOTE: in the grand scheme of things this fantastic fuel altered didn't really have a genuine number as the car was built to show and to bring out at the occasional meetings, with the main aim of showing the crowd the awesome sight of a nitro burning fuel altered. The body for the altered was a replica 1923 turtle deck T. This car brought the art of the fire burnout back to many spectators which provided lots of fun.

1983 Fireworks Meet

A sad meeting and new plain white Houndog 11

The launch of the new Houndog 11 which was left unpainted plain white base coat was saddened for us all as on this last day of the 1983 drag racing season we saw the tragic death of Alan "Bootsie: Herridge, one of the pioneers of the sport in Great Britain.

He was at the time debuting a new jet funny car called Midnight Cowboy which he had built himself. When he made his first full pass it veered left just before the end of the quarter mile, travelling sideways through the timing lights at 140mph hitting the crash barrier head on. The impact was so severe Alan was killed instantly.

Owen and below Alan Bates

1984 November Meet

Owen retires and Alan Bates takes over as the driver of the Houndog 11

All good things have to come to an end and at the end of this season Owen decided to hang up his helmet and Alan Bates replaced him as driver for the Houndog team. Alan was no stranger as he had been part of the team for many years on and off since the seventies and had driven before, but none the less it was quite sad that Owen was giving up but with the usual family commitments he felt the time was right.

And another TV appearance

Childrens TV – Motormouth Corvette Houndog 11

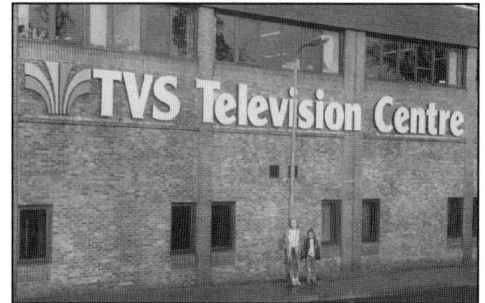

I took Anne, Jodie and Katie to the Motormouth studios. The show was mainly aimed at children and was broadcast live on Saturday mornings. We spent one day rehearsing (the Friday before). Jodie who was very excited about this was allowed to sit in the pods, which were moved around on a fork lift truck, Katie was too young so she stayed with Anne and they watched from the observation room.

Jodie, Charissa (Jodie's best friend) and Katie in a 'pod'

I was interviewed by a very attractive presenter named Andrea Arnold (who also starred in the TV programme No. 73 – she played Dawn). The programme gave us a very good coverage giving the youngsters of the day information about the speed of the car. Andrea, since leaving the programme, now directs tv programmes instead of presentating.

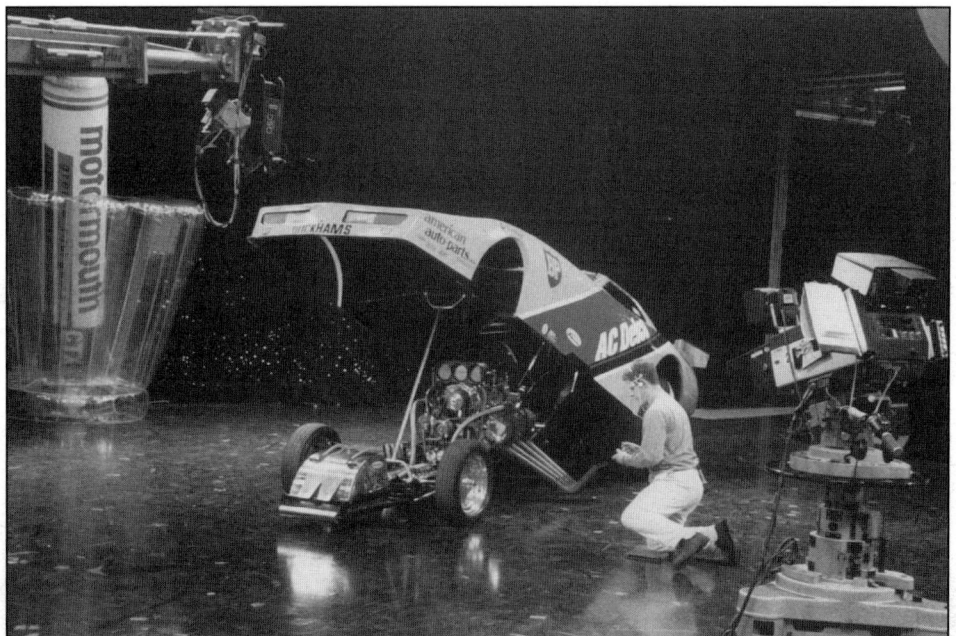

Christian Pamp
Demo's and the funny car

It was during the 80s and we did some demo's with the funny car in Germany and Austria prior to the races at Hockenheim and Austerich ring. On these occasions our crew were able to stay with a German Autoparts supplier, the manager here was Christian Pamp. He was a very likable character and really put himself out in every way to make our stays extremely welcome. We stayed with him many times and he used to crew for me at the race meetings and helped out with our cook-outs and beer at these super events.

When I left drag racing in 1986 I lost contact with him so was very pleased to receive a Christmas card from him and his family twenty odd years on when he relocated to England. We are in contact again and intend to keep it that way.

Here he gives us his experiences and memories:

Nobby called me the other day and asked me to write a few lines for this book. He ended the conversation telling me he can't understand why anybody would want to write a book about him.

Now that's typically Nobby. The only man who doesn't realise that he is his own legend in himself.

I met Nobby in 1986 when I was working for John Woolfe Racing. At the time, I was running the German branch of JWR. Back then, drag racing in

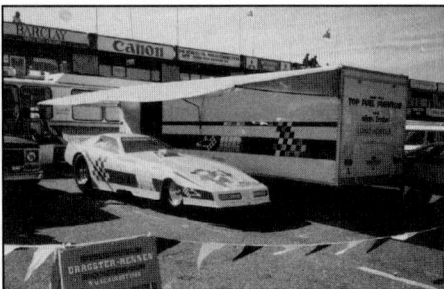

NOBBY'S QUARTER MILE

Germany was just making the transition from a few guys racing their hopped up street cars down the runway of an airstrip, to a full fledged form of motorsport. The first alcohol dragsters and funny cars made the scene. Nitro hadn't arrived yet, save for a few show runs made by Swedish teams.

Enter Nobby Hills with already decades of experience in his pocket and you might be able to imagine what impact he made on the scene. To give our operation some exposure in continental drag racing circles, it was decided that Nobby should campaign his funny car in Europe, and I was supposed to provide assistance should his team require it. Back then, I had little or no exposure to drag racing. I was heavily involved in Stockcar F1 racing and couldn't quite get the point of going down a straight and not turn left at the end.

Well, Nobby did not only manage to change my attitude towards drag racing in one single evening in a pub, he made me an addict for life. His enthusiasm is so overwhelming, that it transpires onto everybody around him. Before you know it, you are involved. See, a nitro-burning funny car not only makes the biggest noise on earth, it also requires constant maintenance.

After each run down the strip, a complete teardown and reassembly is carried out. Fresh fuel needs to be mixed at an eighty-litre a go rate and the most tedious of all things, a chute has to be folded and packed.

On a qualifying day, you do all this four times, which means you slave away from dawn till dusk. If this sounds like an awful lot of hard work, that's exactly what it is. Why would anybody put himself through all this, in high summer, at temperatures approaching 40 degrees?

Well, once you meet Nobby, you'll understand.

After my first encounter with him, I was at least -say- interested. After my first time the thing was fired up next to me, I fully got the message. And after the first time I was out with the gang on the track, saw the car being fired up, doing its burnout and then blasting down 1320 feet of track in less than six seconds, I was unable to stay away from it. Yes, Nobby did put me to work. After all, for an operation like this, you need all the help you can get. But I never regretted it. Nobby never leaves a question unanswered and he never even slightly resists volunteering a piece of his vast knowledge. I learned a lot from him. And not only about funny cars.

Some of the things I learned the hard way. When a meeting was scheduled for Zeltweg in Austria, it was decided to relieve his tow truck of at least some of its burden to cross the Alps to get there.

Thus, four barrels of nitromethane, tyres, oil, and a spare engine block were unloaded onto our trusty Transit company van in Frankfurt. Nobby and his team then set off to Austria and I was to follow, after my workday was over, to join them on Saturday morning. Staying behind with me, and eventually riding shotgun, was one of his team members, Stuart 'Brad' Bradbury.

All went well until we approached the Austrian Border. See, Austria wasn't a member of the EU in those days and there were genuine border controls. Anticipating what lies ahead, I queued in the car lane, in the midst of hordes of tourists, in order to avoid Austrian officials coming too nosey, like they would be over in the truck lane.

NOBBY'S QUARTER MILE

It almost worked. After a glimpse at our passports, the Austrian border policeman was about to let us go. I was already shifting into gear, when I heard the word 'Stop' shouted at me.

'What are these tyres - and what is in these barrels?' 'Uh, erm, officer, these are race slicks for a top fuel funny car and about thousand litres of nitromethane, you know. Why?'

The ensuing discussion lasted two hours. They felt like ten. The result was that "entry in our fine republic" was denied – and a very irritated Santa Pod chief starter.

Now, calling exactly this part of the world home, I knew there were a few tiny little border crossings away from the motorway and chances were good they weren't even manned at 2am on a Saturday.

So back we went into Germany and after an hour of negotiating twisty country roads, we passed a cabin and a sign 'Welcome to Austria'. The cabin was unlit, Austria had us at last. When we arrived at Zeltweg hours late the next morning, we found Nobby worried about our whereabouts. After Brad had told him what happened, we received nothing short of a hero's welcome. That evening, Nobby paid me back with an indecent amount of beer in a local pub.

The entire weekend, Nitro was even more enthusiastically burned than usual, in recognition of the ordeal to get it there.

Nobby has a thing for firing up the funny car in the most unlikely places. One of these was a hall at the Frankfurt exhibition centre, where we set up a stand at a trade fair, using his funny car as a crowd magnet. It took more than a little cajolery to persuade him to refrain from such doings.

When I recently relocated to England, I decided to approach Nobby, after not being in contact with him for more than twenty years. That's when he told me about this book. I'm truly venerated that he asked me to contribute to it.

The two years I was involved with Nobby Hills Racing is a part of my life I don't want to miss. The impact Nobby and his team had on me cannot be overestimated. It was a pleasure and I daresay it changed my outlook on life forever.

People I tell about the times we had back then, often ask me what I feel when I think back. Well, to be honest, I could cry. Nobby Hills is a gentleman, a scholar and an ambassador of top fuel drag racing in Europe.

Christian D. Pamp,

Brian Thomas of Paranoia fame comments on his friendship with Nobby

Over the years drag racing in the UK has produced a number of memorable names Dennis Priddle, Clive Skilton, and Alan Herridge are just a few greats that spring to mind in the fuel car ranks.

However I doubt if the sport ever has, or ever will, produce a more charismatic and flamboyant character than Nobby Hills.

I, myself, started racing in 1975 and he was already a prominent figure in fuel car racing with his front engine rail Houndog, a name that was later to be carried over to several magnificent funny cars as the illustrious career of Nobby progressed.

Back then the competition car ranks was bursting with Jaguar powered cars and I myself ran a comp altered called Paranoia competing in what was classed then as Junior altered.

In those days there were fewer cars that competed on a regular basis but I guess whatever class you competed in we all got to know one another quite well even though we could be poles apart in performance.

Nobby's set up was always a cut above the rest and the standard of turnout was an example of "how it should be done" to all of us.

So, no wonder then that when it came to building a new car I turned to Nobby for some help and advise for the design of the chassis.

Like Nobby, I had always constructed practically

everything on my race cars from the ground up and dare I say it I think he respected that. Appreciating just how difficult it is just to build your own race car on a very tight budget and get it to the track is a mammoth task on its own. Let alone the single minded dedication and determination required to succeed and get to the pinnacle of your class!!!

The standard of workmanship on his cars was practically faultless and perhaps being an engineer I could appreciate the quality and finish more than most.

Of course I never told him that, in fact I was always trying to find fault just to take the Mickey, but I have to confess it was pretty much a hopeless task. In fact he used to give as good as he got when it came to light hearted banter between us regarding who's car was the prettiest and best turned out.

So you can imagine how bold over I was when he invited me over to his workshop to take pictures of a chassis he was building for a new competitor in fuel funny car identical to the one he was currently campaigning.

Not only did he explain in detail how to approach the job but he gave me detailed plans of the most beautiful, modern, trapezoidal chassis in the UK at the time!

Of course I thanked him profusely but assured him with a wry grin that unlike his efforts I would build it properly!

Work progressed on my new Paranoia chassis and the body was to be a unique chopped and lowered Plymouth 5 window coup. The new body proved to be a stunner which could only look right with an ultra low chassis.

NOBBY'S QUARTER MILE

In fact Nobby loved the look of the Plymouth so much he later asked me to make him one for his car.

It looked fantastic with the big blown hemi but unfortunately it was only ever designed with shows in mind, and despite pleads from the adoring fans to "just bring it out for a burnout Nobby", regrettably he never did.

Well in some respects it's a good job he didn't because as it was never intended to be used for racing as I only used a couple of layers of fibre glass.

Although it would have looked fabulous on the track I reckon that at the first hit of the throttle on that awesome motor the whole thing would have disintegrated!

You can imagine my delight when at the first race meeting after Nobby had cast his ultra critical eye over the new car he actually said, "well you ain't made a bad job of it I suppose". To which I replied with a broad grin "well it's a lot better than your attempt at a funny car parked yonder"

After our usual banter had subsided I was immensely proud when he told me what a brilliant job I'd made and that the workmanship and standard of turnout was fantastic. Praise indeed!

The rest is history as they say, and partly due to an excellent chassis design Paranoia went on to be incredibly successful, and I believe the 8.77 at 156mph is still the quickest and fastest mark by a Brit engine altered let alone a Jaguar powered car of any description.

To quote the great man himself, "yeah not bad for

a boat anchor I suppose".

It any sport it seems there are few people that emerge as characters, a true showman, fiercely competitive, but approachable and friendly, with a dry sense of humour. Instantly recognisable to his many adoring fans in his flip flop sandals summer or winter!

I for one am proud to be included in these pages as one of his friends and very excited at the prospect of his return to the sport, after an experience that dare I say it would have probably killed a lesser man!

Nobby has absolutely nothing to prove, his distinguished record speaks for itself having won just about every accolade available in the sport. However, I would like to take the opportunity in these pages to wish my good friend the very best of luck with his beautiful new Funny Car.

Some of the 60 trophies won by the Houndog cars over the years

Like many drag race fans old and new we all look forward to seeing the "New Dog" getting up to his "Old Tricks"

If there had to be only one word I had to use to sum the great man up it would have to be "professional".

Brian Thomas

1986 – 25th May 4.00pm

A Europe's first 5 second run

Certificate of Speed
SANTA POD RACEWAY
Bedfordshire   England
DATE 25 May '86 TIME 16.01   AM/PM
RACE No. AFC 1   ELAPSED TIME 5.99
TERMINAL SPEED 251.8

At this weekend meeting the Corvette Houndog 11 was to become the first British built car to run five seconds ET. This was done with Alan Bates at the wheel, the set up as far as I can remember was a single mag, a single fuel pump which was a 175 Hilborn and the 8.71 blower. This was a good set up for me.

The fuel load was in the region of 84%. We knew this was a going to be a good pass as things had been looking better all weekend. It was around 4.00pm in the afternoon and we did the usual start line routine, I brought Alan into stage, the engine was sounding real crisp, the car left the line instantly, no tyre spin and incredibly straight, I looked down the straight at Santa Pod the lights came on giving a terminal speed of 251.8 and that magical ET of 5.90 seconds. I'd finally achieved something I had set out to do.

After this run, there was much disbelief about the five second run, with all the usual British comments that the timing lights must have been out. I was becoming very concerned and as I later found out so was the RAC. So they took it upon themselves to have the timers checked. We were informed that the checking would happen on the Monday morning, so we stayed at the track and as Monday dawned the RAC people arrived. I was obviously very keen to hear what they found, to my relief the boss man confirmed there was nothing wrong, the timers and speed recorders

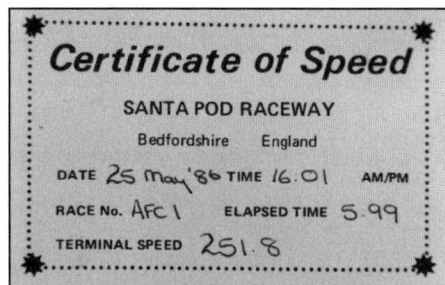

Barry Sheene

Whilst demonstrating at Donnington Park I met Barry Sheene. He was most confused about how we drove our dragsters in respect of the fact there was no clutch pedal but soon understood when I explained how we just selected forward and reverse due to the centrifugal clutch.

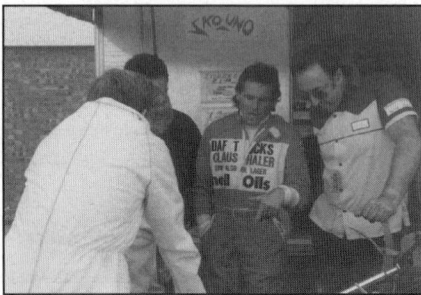

Nobby and Barry Sheene

were perfect. With the RAC present we decided to do it all again for them, so we strapped Alan in to the Corvette and was indicated to proceed. Alan did his typical burnout, plenty of smoke, I lined Alan up into stage, as there was not any safety equipment, we quickly decided against a full pass, a half pass was then started, which recorded a 7.8 sec ET at 130mph, I went up the track in the support truck, where we were waiting for the chute to come out, I suppose at a good half mile beyond the end, the RAC man complete with deerstalker and walking stick had run all the way up the strip, asked if all was alright, and he then exclaimed, "I have never seen anything like that before!" I then enquired what our 0 to 60 times were and he verified that we reached 60mph in .83 seconds. He then explained they had put speed indicators every two feet up the strip for 200ft. The Funny Car had reached 100mph in 72ft from a standstill. Yes it was the first 5 second Nitro Funny Car run in Europe and Scandinavia and proven!

I suppose now that I had achieved what I had set out to do, soon after this I decided drag racing had been possibly ruling my family's life for quite a few years and now perhaps for a while I would step down and semi-retire from this most enjoyable hobby. I had been made redundant and now set myself up as self-employed so consequently I had lots of work commitments and with two daughters and a lovely wife my life was always going to be busy and you can read further on how I filled my time.

1987 ... A new idea

What no Shunter – there is no need to bend for a friend!

I designed and manufactured "The Shunter". This was a special starter trolley for go-karts. It was carefully calculated geometry that carried the kart clear off the ground allowing maximum pushing power at all times from a standing position. This in simple terms stopped the back-breaking part of bending to get a kart started. It was made by a simple lever action that lowered the kart, and still maintained the maximum push. When the engine fired the kart was able to pull away unhindered. The Shunter was made of tubular construction with a zinc coating to resist corrosion. It was a two wheeled trolley with a couple of hooks to slip over the rear bumper. The handle was arranged so that it fell at a natural height for pushing.

I applied for a patent and sold these by advertising in the Kart & Superkart magazine for £45.00 + VAT. Although it was claimed to be the best thing to happen to Class 1 Karting and a very good idea, from my own point of view we only sold a few hundred which was not really enough, if I am honest, to be a successful business on its own, so I decided to discontinue it and carry on with my self-employment welding and fabrication, etc.

It was however well received and mentioned in many magazines and also in Motoring News June 10th 1987 quoted:

Nobby with the Shunter

Starting: a pushover!

Nobby Hills Racing of Biggleswade, Bedfordshire, has come up with a novel idea as a starting aid for 100cc karts, which will eliminate all that back-breaking work countless people have experienced in the past. Called 'The Shunter' the product is of precision-made high quality tubing, and hooked onto the rear bumper of the kart, elevating the rear wheels clear off the ground, allowing easy pushing from a standing position. A quick release handle then drops the kart back up to the surface. Once the engine fires up, the kart moves off unhindered. This product carries a 'Patent Numbers Applied For Classification' and has been extensively tested at several venues during recent weeks.

1985-1989 Association with John Woolfe Racing

It seems most people were under the impression we as a team were sponsored by John Wolfe Racing. This was not so. It was just that at this particular time (1985) I had to move the car from Hatfield and we were allowed to store the car only at the premises of John Woolfe Racing at Bedford. The truck and trailer remained at JMJ Potton. This continued for approximately three years.

During this time I did meet some very genuine people for instance: Arnold Burton, Jill Cole, Ian Messenger, Dennis Stanley, President of Express Parts, Ohio and the lads that worked for John Woolfe Racing at that time.

Later on I went to the States to look at John Lombardo's funny car which was eventually imported into the UK and I then carried out work on it. I modified the chassis and wheelie bar, built the engine, clutch transmission, reverser, pistons, rods, etc. I then took the car to Millbrook test track where we did an awesome burnout in the sunshine with header flames 8ft above the roof.

Dennis Stanley and Nobby

Following this period of semi-retirement I finally decided to sell my truck and trailer and finish with the sport as I had home improvements to concentrate on. The Corvette Houndog car was sold to Martin Hannis and Pete Barnett who converted it to alcohol and I don't think it ran again.

Building the garage at home Anne on the digger!

1990s onwards ...

With more time to spare after totally finishing with my drag racing and not getting involved with building engines for a while it was time to do some different building. The bungalow where we lived required a loft conversion which I was able to build myself and gave us much more room as the family was growing up. I also extended it with a big double garage.

It was at this time I purchased my Silverado pick up truck and we had a touring holiday of the West Country. Travelling was always great fun for us all and for the next couple of years we visited the Canaries, travelled again to the States including Vegas, Los Angeles, West Coast, Phoenix and visited Niagara Falls in Canada which made for a very exciting and enjoyable time for me and my girls.

Jodie and Katie above in the West Country and below at Niagara Falls

All smiling enjoying family life

NOBBY'S QUARTER MILE

The trips to America had influenced my daughters with their love of country sounds and line dancing and it was at this time we started going to Western Dancing. (Read more about this in the article on Jodie).

Work wise I started as a Consultant Manager with Allied Construction Equipment Ltd. Even then travelling still came into the equation and I visited Sweden and also went on a trip on the Orient Express to Ascot. I stayed working with Allied and enjoyed the work of repairing and modifying construction equipment until my accident in 1998.

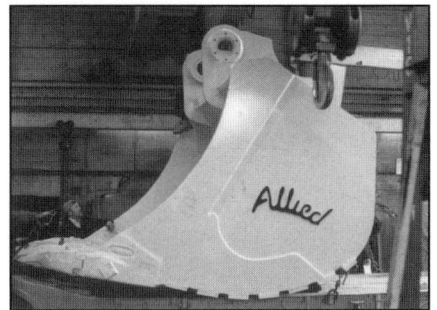

Jodie in the NASCAR Cafe

Below Richard Petty's Plymouth

Jodie with one of the Nashville Speedway Silverados

Katie with Cowboy in Nashville

Jodie and Katie and Cowboy in the Wild Horse Saloon

1995 ...

This was the year that sadly my mother died. She had reached the grand old age of 89 years, and had been a great fan of my "Houndogs" and was quite proud of my achievements although she found it hard to understand why people needed to go quite so fast!

Nobby's mum proudly wearing his Stetson

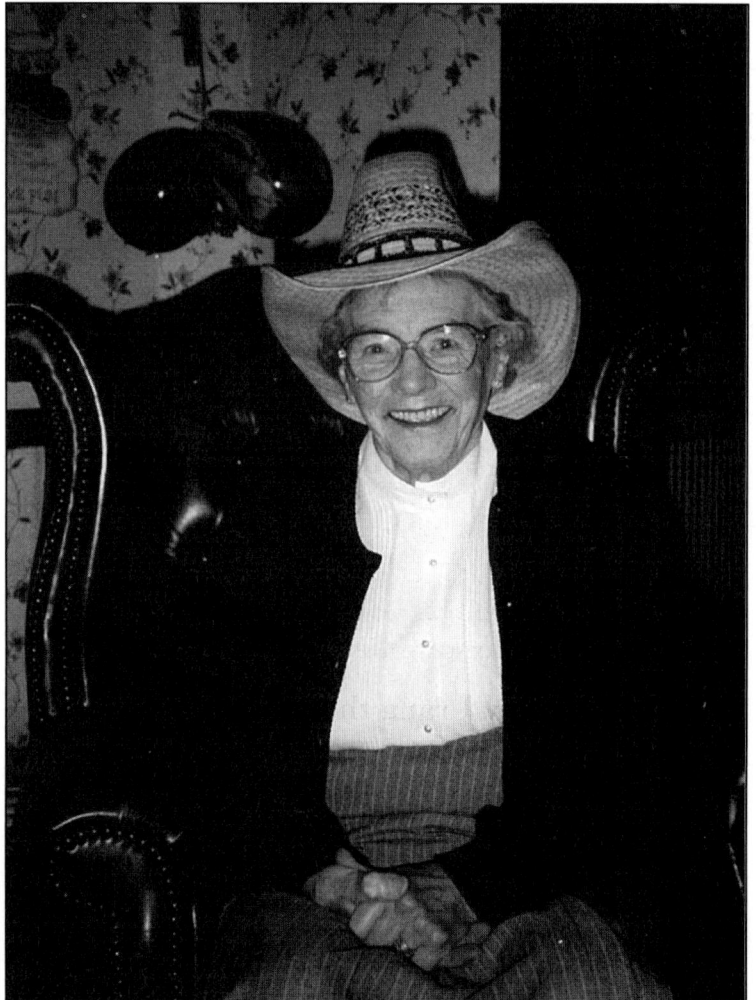

1996–1997 ...

My youngest daughter – Katie Jo

Katie Jo

Katie Jo, my younger daughter, grew up with a great love of art from her first day at school, where she proudly drew a picture of her favourite toy for her teacher, to the current time in 2007 where she obtained a diploma in Art with a triple distinction.

But at thirteen years of age Katie had a little problem when she became very worried about going to school. This came up quite suddenly as prior to this she never had any problems about school and always enjoyed going. After about ten days of repeatedly not wanting to go to school I realised I would have to speak to her alone and find out exactly what was bothering her.

It came out that she was under great pressure from some of the other kids to start glue sniffing during the breaks and lunchtime. I told her that she need not worry and she would not have to go to school any more. To say that I was annoyed would be an understatement.

The following day I rang the school and informed the Principal that Katie would not be attending school from this particular date. Oh dear didn't they make a fuss. Basically they said that it was the law and at her age Katie must attend school and that they would be reporting this to the authorities and that I must expect a visit from the education authorities. By this time in the conversation I was a little more annoyed, I asked them to inform the authorities to make sure whoever came to see me was well armed. They asked why. I said because I

have a piece of four by two timber about 4 foot long by the front door to greet them with. Referring to the conversation about the law and mandatory school attendance I asked them to mention to the authorities that they were allowing glue sniffing to take place during school hours.

This must have done the trick, three weeks after my phone call to the Principal Katie was having home tuition. This continued and she was able to take all her exams at home with very good results.

She finished her education with flying colours and started college to learn to be a beautician and then went on to be an art student. I must add she loves country music and was teaching line dancing from the age of twelve.

She works at the local garden centre and restaurant as well as attending college to further her education in the arts.

I know by taking this decision it helped her enormously as I cannot stand bullying and will always, as most people realise who know me, stand up for my rights for myself and my family at all time. Some call me stubborn and pig headed but sometime these things have to be done.

Elwood the beagle

Katie had also fallen in love with Rosco (Jodie's dog) so after lots of discussions she got a dog of her own, a beagle. This presented another problem, the name for him, as at the time she liked the Blues Brothers, the choice was obvious Elwood Jay Blue, yes he is called Elwood!

Katie Jo ...

What she says about her Dad

The smell of burning rubber and the ear blistering roar of nitro guzzling engines are just two of my earliest and greatest memories. Nope, I was no ordinary kid playing in the back yard with her Barbie dolls. Instead, my sister Jodie and I would be found playing in the pits of drag strips over Europe and Scandinavia, and this could only be down to one person, my dad.

Right from when I was young, as far back as I can remember, I've always thought of my dad as being almost superhuman or even a mad drag racing scientist who builds these weird and wonderful mechanical contraptions.

To me he was capable of anything. If I wanted a complicated shelving unit or a 5 foot high steel bed frame so I could have two floors in my room (no joke, that was certainly real), my dad could make it. If it was dreamable, it was do-able. Of course I would have to be a bit mad myself to suggest these things in the first place but it's obvious who I take after. (I even have vague memories of him mentioning that he was going to build a speedboat with an old Buick engine.)

It was his simple saying "there's no such word as can't", which really inspired me growing up. The drive and enthusiasm that he always puts into his work no matter what job he's doing, has influenced me greatly and when I'm building or welding at college I'm always pleased to say "my dad taught me that!"

He's never been a bog standard, run-of-the-mill

Drag racing painting by Katie Jo and below a small Katie Jo in The Challenger

dad that's for sure, and I'm glad of that. As for him now, he's still going, still crazy and I still think he's INVINCIBLE. An army would struggle to keep him down. Having said that he has gone arse over head a couple of times after a few beers and one of these days I'll get that on camera!

Katie Jo xx

Katie proudly shows off her tattoo of a dragon fly – in memory of her sister Jodie as it was their favourite. After Jodie's death when Katie, Anne and Nobby were visiting New York, a dragon fly was seen flying past them at the statue of Liberty which was very comforting for the family to think that Jodie was still with them

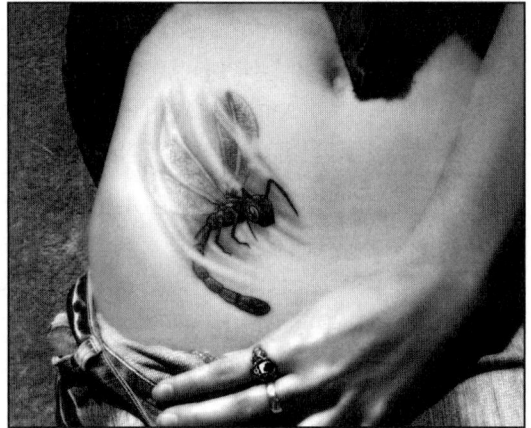

Nobby's girls: Jodie, Grandad (Anne's father) and Katie-Jo

1998 ...

Difficult times ahead

5 days before Christmas and a terrible accident

I was asked by a company to quote for cutting one end out of five 45 gallon drums. I was given the job to do, on the proviso that they were brand new and perfectly clean and the job would be carried out on their premises and with them to supply the gasses.

I went to their factory on the 20th December and proceeded to cut out the drum ends. I got to about drum number four and that is the last I remember of that day. I now know that there were some thinners left in this drum so when I proceeded to cut out with oxy-acetylene there was an enormous explosion and the bottom of the drum took the shape of a large football, the drum left the floor catching me underneath the chin and going about another three metres partially through the workshop roof.

I regained consciousness some weeks later in the intensive care ward of the hospital. My surgeons report tells a story here. I was very fortunate to have the best medical expertise available and thankfully I survived with the support and love of my family.

After many procedures taking place I eventually was allowed home in February. Here I had to learn most things again including walking, but I was determined and I made it. It took me nearly three years. I must say that the hospital staff were wonderful and Dr. Anna my G.P. was absolutely superb and I cannot thank them all enough for my gift of life.

Nobby fabricating exhaust systems

Nobby is one of the few people outside of the USA who is a member of SEMA which is the Speciality Equipment Manufacturers Association

Fighting for life ...

This has kindly been written by Michael T Simpson BDS MBBS MRCS FFDRCS Consultant Oral & Maxillo-Facial Surgeon who helped 'put Nobby together again'

Nobby's memories of this event are still a bit patchy with the severity of the accident so he is very grateful to Michael for helping out in more ways than one.

On 20th December 1998, Nobby suffered an explosion to the face and was brought as an emergency by ambulance to the Accident & Emergency Department of the Lister Hospital in Stevenage.

Apparently, he had been opening an industrial barrel of paint when it exploded in his face. Having ricocheted off his face, it went upwards through the roof of the building and the blow knocked him backwards so that he struck the back of his head with some force against a brick wall. He was bleeding profusely from the mouth and nose when seen and because of the extent of swelling, couldn't open his eyes. His airway was compromised and because of the difficulty in breathing and oxygenating his blood, intubation was attempted. Because of the extent of haemorrhage and the restricted airway, the tube could not be safely introduced to his upper airways and so an emergency tracheostomy was performed.

Further resuscitation was performed and then he was immediately taken to the CT scanner to obtain X-ray pictures of his brain, skull and the facial bones. These showed that he had fractured the back of his skull in several places. There was a fracture on the right of his skull with some extradural bleeding just above his brain. There was further swelling on the right side of his brain.

Extensive facial fractures were noted and most of his sinuses were full of blood. The floating bone in the neck called the hyoid bone was also fractured and there was displacement of his pharynx and airway to the right side.

Because he had been opening a paint barrel, following the explosion he was plastered with bits of very hot paint and this meant that on top of his other injuries, he had paint burns to his body but mainly on his legs.

In terms of the fractures of his facial bones, most of these were in fact fractured. There was a comminuted fracture of his mandible meaning that the bone was broken in lots of pieces in one part. There were bilateral fractures of his jaw joints. There was a fracture of his nose and the bones either side of his nose and there were fractures of the middle-third of his facial skeleton at what we call the Fort I, II and III levels. This was associated with orbital floor fractures, which is the bone under his eyes, and on the left side the lower rim around the eye was fractured in several places.

He was admitted to the Intensive Care Ward for further observation and resuscitation and was transfused with two units of blood because of the blood that he had already lost. Many teeth had been blown out of their sockets and three of these had been inhaled into his lung. After a period of time, a further CT scan of his brain was undertaken to check that there was no deterioration with regard to his brain injury and fortunately for Nobby, there wasn't.

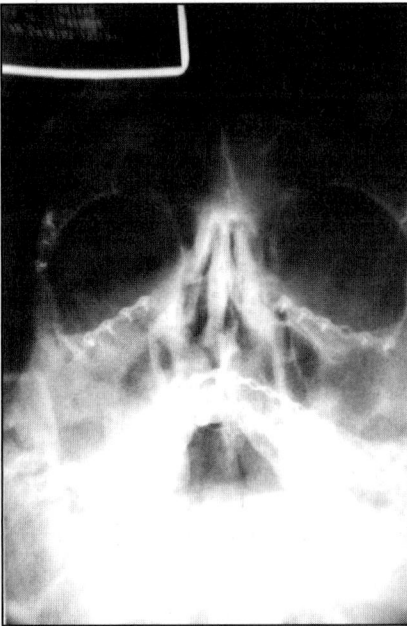

X-rays showing the extent of Nobby's reconstruction

Picture clearing showing the massive fracture to Nobby's skull

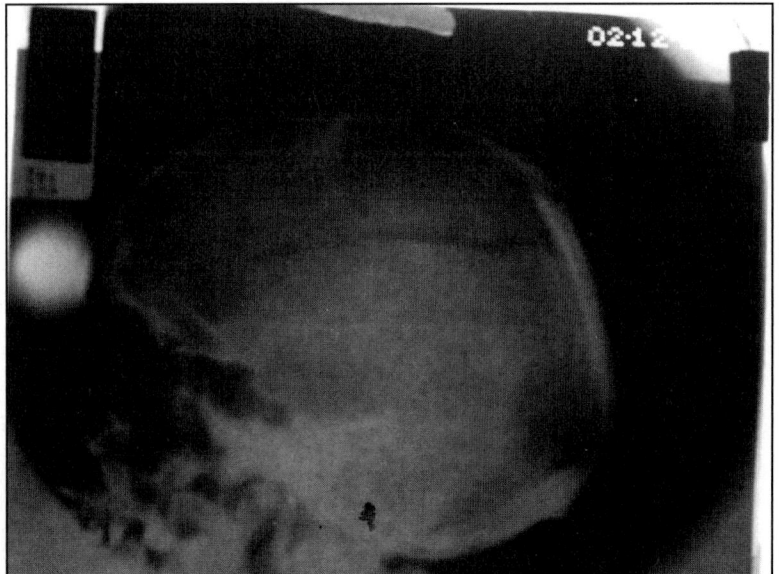

Four days after his admission and following a conversation with Mr. Rees, Consultant Cardiothoracic Surgeon at Harefield, he was taken into the operating theatre and anaesthetised. Mr. Rees, Consultant Cardiothoracic Surgeon managed to remove two incisor teeth from the left lower part of his lung. A piece of broken denture was also removed from the right lung. However, there was a further fragment of tooth on the right side which he was unable to remove because of the anatomy and technical difficulties.

Under the same general anaesthetic, his mouth and broken jaw was debrided and multiple pieces of bone fragment and paint removed. Four titanium bone plates and some wires were used to reduce his mandibular fractures. His middle-third of face fractures were repaired and immobilised using further titanium plates. Bars were attached to his remaining upper and lower teeth so that they could splint each other and the upper bar had a projection from the mouth which could be fixed to his skull to help provide immobilisation later on if necessary. Both of his cheek bones were repositioned into the correct position and further bone plates used to secure them to the front of his skull. The bone under his eyes was explored and repaired. On the left side, the orbital rim of bone under the eye was comminuted and this was repaired with mini plates made of titanium. His nasal fractures were reduced and the bones held in alignment by using plates with what we call transfixion wires between them. Pins were placed into the front orbital region of his skull to support a frame which was connected to the projection bar secured to his upper jaw so that his upper jaw could be held rigidly upwards and forwards. His wounds were cleaned and many sutures placed, the whole procedure taking approximately seven hours.

What a way to spend Christmas Eve!

Whilst Nobby was still anaesthetised, because he would have trouble with swallowing and eating for some time to come and because we couldn't pass a tube properly through his mouth or his nose into his stomach, a gastrostomy feeding tube was placed through his abdomen into his stomach. Once again under the same general anaesthetic, the burns on his legs were thoroughly cleaned and debrided and a skin graft was taken from his right thigh to resurface the biggest area of burnt skin.

Nobby in Intensive Care

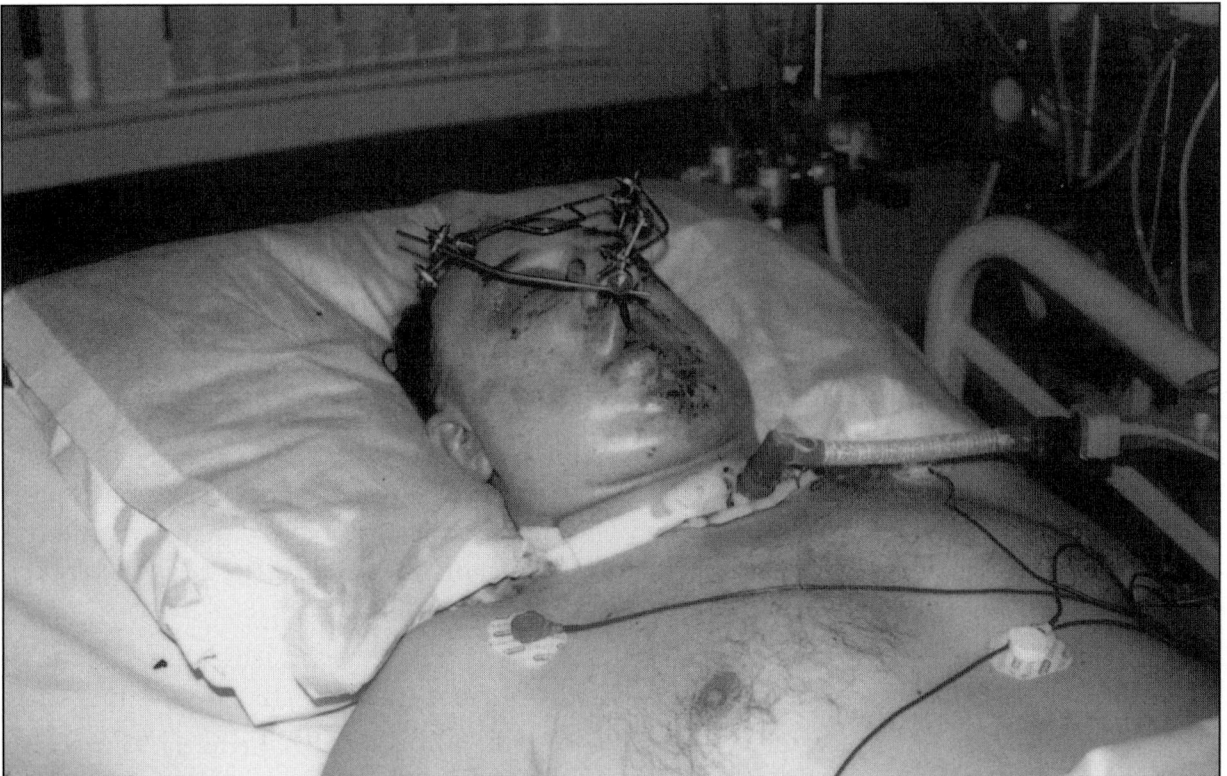

After this major operation, Nobby had a number of problems. First of all, he became infected with the so-called superbug MRSA but fortunately this was controlled with antibiotics. Also, his blood pressure became quite high and difficult to deal with. Fortunately within two weeks, he was picking up with increasing speed.

His nasal splints were removed on 4th January 1999 and by the 18th day, he was able to move his feet, legs, arms and was in fact discharged from the Intensive Care Unit to the ward on 8th January. The rods and bars connecting his upper jaw to his skull were removed on 15th January.

By 4th February, we had removed some wires from his mouth and he was discharged home, having also recovered from a urinary tract infection probably as a result of being catheterised for so long, on 9th February. He slowly made progress at home but unfortunately developed a thrombosis of his left leg and was re-admitted shortly on 29th April and put on Warfarin (rat poison!).

Some six months later when he had come off Warfarin, I referred him back to the Cardiothoracic Surgeon, Mr. Rees, who on 12th November 1999, managed to remove the last tooth from his right lung which he recovered very well from.

He required numerous visits to several out-patient departments, including Maxillo-Facial Surgery, General Surgery, Neurology and Plastic Surgery, who all played a part in his treatment and rehabilitation.

Since that time, he has also had one further plate removed from his jaw with a very short admission and my wife has managed to provide him with new dentures to try and restore his good looks!

From my point of view, Nobby has always dealt with his injuries with great fortitude and a smile and it has been a privilege to treat him and to also have met his family.

Naturally, I was very upset when he lost his daughter following a road traffic accident. I think it is true to say that Nobby's treatment was a real team event and it is difficult to appreciate looking at his face as it is today the extent of these injuries because he is just as ugly as usual!

Michael T Simpson BDS MBBS MRCS FFDRCS

Consultant Oral & Maxillo-Facial Surgeon

Nobby's reply ...

When you're ugly like me

You jes naturally gotta be cool!

December 1998 ...

After the accident

After my accident I made a very progressive recovery, it did take a very long time, about four years in total, the only time I have ever had off work was about 1959 when I was a week out after a hospitalised football injury, so having a long time out did not really suit me at all. I really felt frustrated not being allowed to do very much at all. I am sure the medical advise I received was very good. Anyway I suppose I drove Anne, Jodie and Katie nearly round the bend.

My recovery involved, over a period of time, lots of hospital outpatient visits, specialist hospital visits and dentistry work. Here I would like to thank all those involved.

My Dentist ...

Dr. Ann Simpson

My surgeon suggested specialist dental work as my mouth had taken quite an impact during the accident and my teeth certainly needed sorting out, especially as some had ended up in my lung. So I finished up approaching The Bedford Dental Surgery who were happy to take me on as a patient and I made an appointment to see a Dr. Ann Simpson, yes she was non other than the wife of my Surgeon, Mr. Michael Simpson. After the initial visit I went back about two weeks later. I think I hold the record for time in the dentist chair, it worked out to be three hours and twenty minutes! She had to undertake a great deal of work in my mouth on this occasion. I guess it was needed and when she was finished – she stood back looked at me and said "I don't know about you Mr. Hills but I'm totally knackered!" This made me laugh and since this visit I have had regular visits for treatment and I feel she has done me proud and from a patient's point of view I can say I think she is brilliant; the only dentist I have been able to chat to and with the ability to give me an injection virtually without feeling anything at all. Thank you very much Dr. Ann.

Harefield Hospital ...

Visiting Mr. Rees

I had a follow up visit to Mr. Rees regarding the last tooth left in my right lung. For this I travelled to Harefield Hospital. On entering Mr. Rees surgery office I was greeted by Mr. Rees and told to sit down and the usual procedure – how are you? etc. Followed by I thought I had better see how this lost tooth, or part of it that's still in your lung is.

So I asked the obvious question, "can you tell me why you didn't remove it when you removed the rest?" He shook me a little with is answer. He said, "because you were going to bloody well die!" You know I am very nervous when I am in a hospital and particularly in this situation, then the next thing he said really frightened me.

He said, "now you have a real problem", that was about all I needed, I think I could have gone to the loo at this time. The look on his face didn't say anything sympathetic and I said to myself "stand up and be counted boy!"

I then said to Mr. Rees, "OK tell me all about it then". He said, "the problem is you proved me wrong in front of everyone" and he then actually smiled and continued, "that's it I'll give you a call in about seven days time, come down and I'll remove this last piece". I was told by my surgeon Mr. Simpson that this man was a real character with a wry sense of humour and he sure is. Not that this story ends yet as I think I was a match for him with my own sense of humour.

Sure enough within ten days he telephoned me at

home and told me to be at Harefield on 12 November 1999. I turned up and was given a bed in the ward. I was dressed up in the theatre operation gear and waited to be taken to the theatre. The nurse then asked me if I had brought my x rays down from the Lister hospital in Stevenage. I had not done so, I was then told by the nurse that I had better get dressed and go home and another time would have to be arranged. She then went off to tell Mr. Rees of the situation. I started to change again then all of a sudden the nurse returned, she said it was OK to get back into the hospital gear again. I of course asked what exactly was happening to which she informed me that Mr. Rees didn't need the x rays as he knew precisely where the tooth was. This naturally made me tremble at the mere thought but by then the porters arrived to take me down to the theatre. Now Mr. Rees was standing in the corridor, he was all dressed up ready to operate, so when I was close to him he said, "how's things?" to which I replied, "great but one thing I want is when you get this tooth out I would like to keep it." He enquired as to why I would want it so I jokingly told him, "I want to take it to my dentist and get it put back in my mouth". So he told me "fine" and then went off into the theatre. Some hours later I came round in the recovery ward and strapped to my chest with sticky tape was a large hospital type bucket with a label on it saying Nobby's tooth.

After a hospital rest I returned home to Biggleswade clutching the tooth. Well I carefully cleaned it, I then bought some clear plastic two pack, and being a country boy I found an old belt buckle. I then, without Anne knowing, borrowed one of her best dessert spoons and moulded the tooth into the clear cast and fixed it to the buckle and it doesn't look bad at all.

The belt buckle with the tooth in

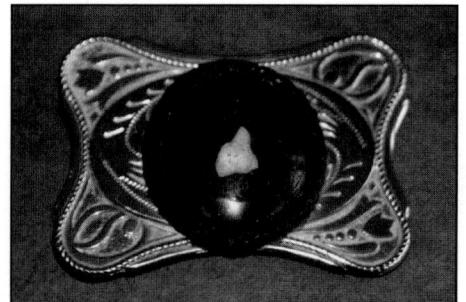

Next month I had to visit Mr. Rees for a check up. I obviously wore jeans, boots and belt buckle. When I entered his office he immediately asked if I had got the tooth put back, to his surprise I said yes, I then showed him my belt buckle. His reply was, "I just can't believe you Mr. Hills".

All I can say is here's another fantastic person who helped me get back to normal and I would just like to say another big thank you Mr. Rees.

1999 ...

Fortitude of life

This has kindly been written by Anna Zahorski Nobby's GP whose help and understanding in difficult times has been invaluable to him.

Nobby Hills – drag racing legend

It was only fairly recently that I understood this about Nobby Hills. What I know about drag cars would not cover a postage stamp. What I know about Nobby's humanity would cover pages – and is why I feel qualified to contribute to this book.

I met Nobby and his family in 1999, when I became his GP in his home town.

I am not sure if I met him prior to his industrial accident. I do re-call his family talking of his progress whilst he was still in hospital. It was a hard time for all of them – life/death issues inevitably are. The thing that shone through – and remains in my mind all these years on – was their love, their family unity. They were as one.

One day – there he was. He came to tell me of how it had been, what had happened, the treatments he had been through and those that were planned. All I had received from the hospital were medical reports full of jargon.

Hearing about it from Nobby himself made me understand the severity of his injuries and painted a graphic picture of the personal impact. He was so very aware of how lucky he was to be alive.

Despite the horrendousness of it all, the one outstanding thing was Nobby's attitude. It soon became apparent he had total respect and implicit faith in his surgeon and medical staff. He believed, that as highly qualified and well respected professionals in their field, they knew what they were about. He allowed them to get on with rebuilding his body with the utmost of faith. For his part, he co-operated and complied with all of their suggestions. Working together, they put Nobby back together again.

The privilege of being a GP is that, if allowed, relationships can be formed through shared experiences, providing tremendous bonds for the ones waiting to trip us up as part of our destiny.

So it was, that when I learnt of the tragic loss of his daughter Jodie in a road accident, I knew that Nobby and I had already cemented the foundations of our relationship. I trusted that they would be solid enough for us all.

For many weeks, I sat with him, Anne and Katie, witnessing their searing pain. His initial belief, crippling paralysis, total devastation. As time went by and we sat together, I often wondered what they were wanting and needing me to provide. Was it the role of 'Doctor', 'Healer personified', 'Girl with the Magic Wand'?

I felt hopelessly inadequate.

Ultimately all I could bring, so willingly, was myself. To be alongside them as they went through the darkest journey of their lives.

After each visit I returned to my car. Nearly 30 years of doctoring and human tragedy. Still – with Nobby, every time, tears escaped me before I felt able to move.

Nobby continued to talk to me over the years, telling me of his struggle to know what had happened to Jodie in the accident. The why, the how? His relentless pursuit to know the events of her final moments – to really know, in the spirit of justice. To do right by and for his child.

As time has gone on, Jodie's name is never far from his lips. Whether spoken or not, I can always feel his pain.

We are told that out of tragedy something is born. If Jodie's death was Nobby's personal crucifixion, then her living spirit, the love of his family and friends together with those of complete strangers, are his resurrection.

I have known Nobby for many years now – and have witnessed first hand his integrity and honesty, as well as his respect and valuing of others. It is however his exemplary commitment to his Jodie and his family that have moved me to the core.

I was totally overwhelmed by Nobby wanting me to be in his biography. However, I welcomed the opportunity to express how knowing him has touched me in a way that is only explicable through the mystery of being human. For this – and to Jodie – I shall always be grateful.

So – if Nobby were ever to say to me, 'Anna get in that Houndog and do a lap at Santa Pod', I would raise a few eyebrows.

The answer would have to be 'yes of course, Nobby.

But ... he would have to come with me!

So I hope that I will continue the privilege of sharing Nobby's journey on this complicated road called life.

Anna Zahorski.

Drag racing reunion

5 June 1999

The first drag racing reunion was organised by myself, Jodie and Alan Bates. It took place at the Weatherley Centre, Biggleswade. This was a great event with one hundred plus cars and bikes on show. The Commuter was also here on the day, kindly brought along by Anthony Billinton and the Golden Rod was bought along by US Automotive. Anglia TV filmed the event and Jodie had a line dancing display with lots of country music being played. The day was a very special event and I think helped with my decision about the future.

THE FIRST REAL
DRAG RACERS RE UNION
HOT CARS AND DRAG RACING STARS
COUNTRY AND ROCK 'N' ROLL PARTY
SAT JUNE 5th '99
THE WEATHERLEY CENTRE, BIGGLESWADE, BEDS
LARGE SCREEN VIDEO PROJECTION SYSTEM
2000 WATTS PER CHANNEL OF
HOT COUNTRY MUSIC AND THE BEST ROCK 'N' ROLL
BY KJ's COUNTRY SOUNDS
Organised by JODIE'S COUNTRY,
ALLAN BATES and NOBBY HILLS RACING
Air-conditoned bar facilities and trade stands
ALL DAY FROM 10am
Everyone welcome
Tickets in advance £5.00
Children under 14 free !
01767 314106 / 01763 220744
It's ATTITUDE that counts and WE know it

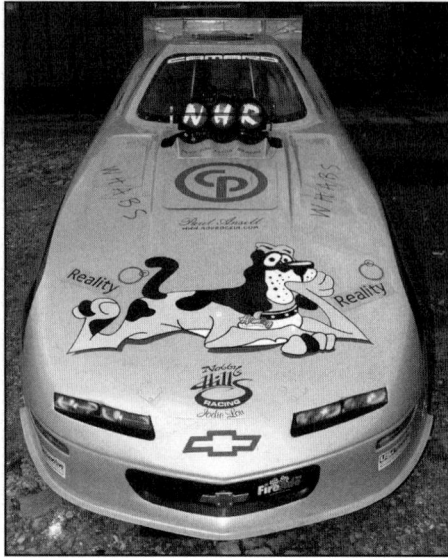

Houndog 12

Thoughts on a new Houndog ...

Houndog 12 on the way

I am not a lazy person and one day, as my recovery was well on the way in 2001, I had a few words one morning within the four of us about not being allowed back at work and not doing anything really positive. Anne and Jodie then went out for a day of shopping as girls do. I was getting beyond a joke to live with I suppose. At this particular time I decided to build another funny car. I was fed up watching all my cars on video and looking in my scrap books and at all the old photographs. I needed a goal and something to get me going so the decision was made. Most people said that's a big one to make at your age! My reply was always, "well 28 years is just the age to start again especially with a little experience!"

Well the girls came back from the shops and enquired if I was feeling better and I informed them I was feeling much better and I told them my news that I was going to build a new funny car. Anne immediately said to Jodie jokingly, "we should have pulled the tubes and the wires out and smothered him when we had a chance in intensive care! I am sure glad they didn't.

I could not wait to get started. I suppose this was just what I needed. So the planning stage quickly began with the chassis. This was fairly easy for me as having built 27 before this I had a rough idea which way to run. I spent about eight weeks drawing the plans for the chassis, as mine tend to be a bit different in some areas as I like to up the specifications a little. I suppose over the years I have learnt many tips to enhance these.

Geoff Hauser helped with the latest chassis spec, i.e. tube, outside diameters, wall thickness, etc. The next thing I did was make a jig. This was the first full jig that I had made to construct a chassis and it worked out very well. One thing I always do with my chassis is mark the side frame tubes so that they can be measured diagonally. This I

Construction under way

did with this chassis and it worked out the best I'd ever made. I guarantee that this one over the full length is less than ten thou out. That's less than ten thousanth's of one inch out of square over the complete full length of the chassis. The rear chassis was welded completely before I acquired a block axle and front wheel set up.

The welding was carried out by a good friend of mine, Gary Dennett, who is a fully qualified aircraft welder, as good as they get. I then acquired a TFX block, Chrisman rear and the McKinney motor plate, front wheels and rear wheels. I was able to make nylon motor bearing locators to allow a 1½ EN24 steel mandrel to line up the motor and the pinion on the rear, as I always do when building my cars. I am sure this is a good reason why they tend to go straight with the pinion being perfectly in line with the main bearing in the block. The drive line coupler just slides in place lovely. The next thing was a replica body. I wanted another Corvette but I couldn't fine one so I went for a Camaro which I quite liked.

I fitted this in my back yard making all new tin work. I had to do this because of my own design chassis. I also moved the engine forward 2 in, there is a good reason for this, the weight transfer when leaving the start line.

I realise this project has taken rather too much time as all my other cars were built in very large workshops with everything I wanted to get the job done, whilst this car was built in my back yard under a car port. As one imagines there is a big difference, but if you want to do something bad enough (as I did) you'll find a way to do it.

When it came to fitting the controls, pedals, steering, fuel shut off, etc. I built everything around my daughter Jodie, her being totally dedicated to drag racing and an average build. It was the thing to do and it worked out very well.

NOBBY'S QUARTER MILE

At about this time I met up with Angelo at Brights of Biggleswade. Angelo allowed the car to be kept in his car showroom and Brights Coachworks did the paint job.

It was now time to think about the parts that make it bark. TFX block, AFT clutch, Trick Titanium Bell Housing, Lenco Reverser, crank, rods and piston etc. There are people here that I must mention, Roy of Homes in the Sun, Warren of Good Fabs, Stuart of US Automotive and Mick of ML Dredging.

Also at this time also I was designing the 40ft trailer. I also needed a larger pick up truck because I was in favour of a swan neck. I built the trailer and then acquired the pick up. A wonderful help here was Mick of Ware Heating and Bathroom Supplies.

The car was unveiled at the NEC 2004 courtesy of Custom Car Magazine. They had already done a five page feature on the car and I felt a little honoured by this.

Comments included:

The long anticipated wait for the new car from Nobby Hills is over. Looking fantastic in its colour scheme, the car was launched on the Custom Car stand at the Autosports show at the National Exhibition Centre on the 9th January 2004. Nobby is no stranger to the world of funny car drag racing, in fact he is, with his long time driver Owen Hayward, a true icon of European drag racing and has been a major feature on the scene since the sixties.

The new car shows a great promise indeed.

Sandringham Flower Show 2007 from left to right: Duncan, Nobby, Simon (the son of Owen Hayward) and Jez Batch

Sad times ...

Unfortunately shortly after the second show I did, with the car at Xtreme Wheels, Alexandra Palace 2004 my lovely daughter Jodie died. As you can imagine this put a stop to the proceedings in every form and every time I looked at the car I felt Jodie was sitting in it saying things like, "I think the steering should be a little higher or closer". I had to keep away from the car for many months, it was just too painful.

I eventually got back into the project as I know Jodie would have wanted it more than anything. People like Jez and Maggi (Dolphin Graphics) helped a lot with this book and I tell you I needed it, and without Katie and Anne I would not have made it. I feel sure having virtually completed the car I have had many thoughts on how it should run. I have always believed that here in the UK and Scandinavia everything is so different from the USA, air temp and track temp. I think we may have one day per year if we are lucky where we can run the set up. Therefore I have thought out and manufactured my own clutch and fuel control and by spending a week in the States in Los Angeles with Tony Miglizzi and his son Lanny I may have come up with the results.

Nobby at Dolphin Graphics (publishers) with Maggi discussing his book manuscript

I fired the motor up in September 2007 and again in October and November. By the last fire up the car moved under its own power and was barking real loud over these three fire ups. I put forty five gallons of 90% through, obviously a little rich at first but that's what to do initially, run it rich and soft. I am convinced I am on the right lines.

Proud father with Jodie

Sammy Miller's car Oxygen in the pits besides Nobby Hills trailer

Jodie Lou ...

August 24th 1978 – April 7 2004

My first lovely daughter Jodie Lou was born to us on August 24th of this year. She was a lovely baby of 8lbs 7oz with a little blonde fluff on her head.

I remember I used to take Jodie everywhere. I think she first attended SPR at one month old. At a press reception at the Hind Hotel in Northampton Jodie was about six months old I had her in a carry cot, the type that looks a little like a plumbers bag. It had a zip and two handles and I was standing talking to Sammy Miller (the American drag racer who drove the Rocket Car, Vanishing Point and Oxygen) with the bag on the floor between my legs, he eventually said, "what ya got in the bag Nobby?" I replied, "Sammy there's a baby in there", to which he retorted, "no way!" So I bent down and unzipped the bag. Jodie was at her bottle, Sammy was absolutely thunderstruck and he never forgot about this. Later on when I was invited to Anthony Billinton's fortieth birthday at a restaurant in Rushden, Sammy was also there. When the opportunity arose I walked over and said "Hi Sammy", "Nobby Hills", he replied I know who you are I will never forget the baby in the bag and the lovely blonde Anne. He then asked how Jodie was, I said, "she is fine and told him he could speak to her on my mobile if he wanted. He took this opportunity and spoke on the telephone for about fifteen minutes, I was over the moon and so was Jodie, unfortunately Sammy died on an oil rig a couple of years later.

From the age of six months she would accompany me to the workshop of SLDO every weekend that I was not racing. I would spread a blanket onto the workshop floor with a bed cover on top. She would sit in the centre with her toys, drinks and food. I was then able to work on my race project. Having one or two race cars I would very often go on European trips to shows all over. The Silverado truck was equipped with a recliner type child seat which was strapped in the middle on the front bench seat. Anne and I would change driving almost without stopping the rig, we had it down to a fine art.

Anne with a thirteen year old LeAnn Rimes

On one trip, in our spare time, whilst in Switzerland, we went in a cable car and were able to see over the mountains for miles. It was another wonderful trip for us. These excursions went on for many years including visits all over Europe including Germany, Holland, Sweden, Austria and France.

On a five week break in 1979 we all went to Florida. It was early July and we fell in love with the place. It was there that Jodie took her first steps which to me was such a great thing as I am so American thinking. It was as I remember on a visit to the space centre to see the rocket and space capsules. By this time Jodie could stand up and take a step or two very carefully whilst holding on to something. She was now eleven months old and what do you know there we were looking at the lunar landing module as I was always interested in space travel. I stood near the module to take her picture and then she walked towards me with two or three steps without falling over. I picked her up

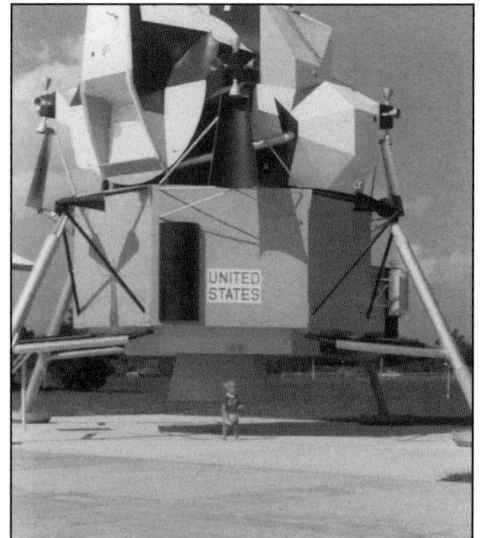

First steps at the space centre

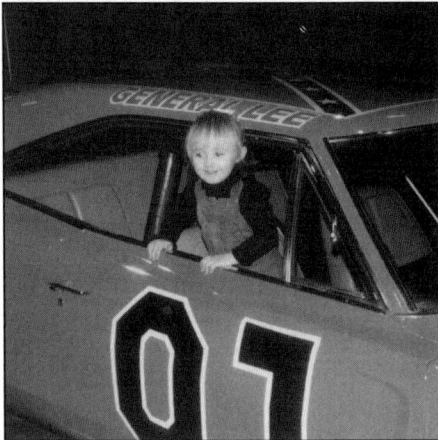

Katie left and Jodie right

and told her how chuffed and proud I was because she had taken her first steps unaided under an American Lunar Module!

When Jodie was three years old I bought her a pedal car and converted it to 12v drive with a windscreen motor which I adapted to power the rear wheels. She drove this around on Santa Pod raceway, she loved this very much.

Jodie's love of the Dukes of Hazard was born when, at about four years old, I was booked to take the funny car to the NEC in Birmingham for a high performance car show and lo and behold also on the display was the original film car for the Dukes of Hazard. As we were there a day early I was able to take a picture of her in the car which she was thrilled with. This was a great moment for us both as we always watched the show on television together, as I still do.

When Jodie was five we had our second daughter Katie Jo. She was absolutely thrilled with her new sister and they became very close over the years and later on both taught line dancing together.

Jodie had been at play school since she was three years and then started normal school at five years old. I went with her on her first day at real school. She did all the normal things all kids do. I had a meeting to discuss with her headmaster the times that she would need to be away when we were at shows or foreign race meetings. His opinion was that he felt it was more beneficial for her to travel with us every time as she would be gaining a lot in travel experience. It was always a concern of mine when we had to go away but racing shows were fantastic during these years and I think Jodie got to know more about drag racing than

NOBBY'S QUARTER MILE

I did at times! It was an unusual way of life but provided my daughters with an alternative form of education, totally unique and full of fun, love and laughter and yes they were weaned on fast cars and country music.

I bought her a Honda trike for her eighth birthday, she was thrilled to bits. She loved to ride this with her crash helmet on and I remember some weeks later I arrived home from work, parked my car in front of the bungalow, got out and then heard the Honda trike come revving down from the top of my backyard. I thought great. Then I saw it, Jodie had her crash helmet on and I had a big shock. Katie my younger daughter was laying on the fuel tank and hanging on like mad. She was only 3½ years old and not dressed for the occasion. I didn't know what to say, they had obviously done this before – there you go that's kids for you.

During these years country music was on all my sound systems and we would play it all the while so both my girls were really into it in a big way as well as drag racing.

Jodie did very well at school, she was always very neat and tidy and often took ever so much trouble to clean my support trucks. She had a cleaning kit, a set of brushes for cleaning the A/C vents, I must admit she kept the truck perfect. Yes, she was never far from trucks and go karts and in her younger years she had seen the best of drag racing in Europe and the UK.

Eight year old Jodie on her trike.

A different way of life for the Hills family with Nobby's retirement from drag racing ...

Never far away were the country sounds and in the middle 80's I was pressed into temporary retirement from drag racing. So in a short period of time Jodie was soon asking, "what are we going to do now dad?". I must admit there was a big gap in our activities, certainly no gap in country music, so well there you go. I phoned up an old acquaintance of mine who ran the Hayriders Country Club in Hemel Hempstead and sure enough he was going strong. So every Friday evening we went to the Hayriders and the first time we were there, we became aware of a group of about six or seven people doing a real different type of modern dancing to country music. They were in fact line dancing. All four of us were really intrigued and we had to find out more. So within a few weeks we had contacted the British Western Dance Association for a line dance teacher so we could learn. We found one and within three months we were all capable of joining in some of the dances on Friday evenings. Anne, Jodie and Katie soon became very good at Western line dancing.

The year was 1992 and Jodie, who was always a very shy young girl, staggered me this year when she said to me she wanted to be a line dance teacher. The facts being she was that shy, she would not answer the telephone, she would not answer the door and always kept away from any visitors who may have called. My reaction to her was simple and I said, "if you won't answer the telephone or the door how on earth are you going to stand up on a stage and possibly teach one hundred or more people to dance?". I could see the potential in Western line dancing and she told me she did not have a problem doing just that. I was so taken aback with her assurance that I booked her on a BWDA dance course and I drove her to Blackpool for this to see for myself. Another young dancer on this dance course was a Mr. Rob Fowler, they both passed with flying colours. Jodie was just fifteen years old at this time. Rob went on to line dance fame. Afterwards Jodie booked the Biggleswade Weatherley Centre one night a week on Mondays. I purchased a complete sound system for her with a radio microphone. I was surprised that on her first night she had fifty seven people in attendance.

She soon introduced line dancing to the Biggleswade, Bedford and Hertford area. The next five or six years were unbelievable for her, she eventually had five different dance classes with live bands on Saturday evenings every week. Her shows in the early and best years consisted of 2 amps of 1000w per channel and a five metre wide video professional system with two cameras putting the foot work on the screen as there were too many people there to be able to see the tough dance steps on the stage – by then Katie had joined Jodie and they both taught using radio microphones.

I felt very proud as it was a professional show. Yes,

they travelled as far as Hatfield and beyond as at the time there were no line dances anywhere like it. It was a very popular craze and Jodie's Country was very much in demand with bookings for weddings, private functions, fetes and charities.

Here are some excerpts from a line dancing article about Jodie and the family:

Imagine growing up with Country Music from an early age. Add the excitement of travelling the world with a drag racing team, and you have a childhood to remember. Jodie and Katie Hills were weaned on fast cars and Country, and now they're setting the pace on the dance floor.

"The drag racing took over everything" recalled Jodie. "We've had drag cars parked down our road." The Hills must have had understanding neighbours, or did they? "No. We had to move out!" replied Jodie with a grin on her face.

For Jodie and Katie, childhood was often spent on the move. Their father's drag racing took them all over Europe to countries including Austria, France,

Above: Alan Jackson and below: Jodie's Country Chevrolet Luminar

NOBBY'S QUARTER MILE

Germany, Holland and Sweden. Although the drag racing calendar sometimes coincided with the school term, the girls' travels provided them with a fine alternative education and country music was always on the syllabus. "We travelled the world in a 16 metre long Chevrolet truck and trailer fitted with a sound system which rejected anything that wasn't Country Music", quipped Nobby.

Country is never far from Jodie's thoughts. "The artists can sing", she explained "and there's often a story-line in Country music. All the singers have characters and like my dad I'm a big fan of Alan Jackson, Brookes and Dunn, George Jones and Waylon Jennings", Jodie also named Patty Loveless, LeAnn Rimes and Sara Evans among her favourite female performers.

Jodie's belt and buckle which she was very proud of and wore all of the while when she taught line dancing

When Nobby retired from drag racing, leaving a gap in the family's lives, by happy coincidence the Hills discovered Line Dancing in the country clubs at the same time and it did change their lives. The family immediately felt at home line dancing, for as Jodie says, to be a good line dance or drag racer, you need straight lines!

During Jodie's line dance club Anne and Nobby lend a hand "some other dance classes do well with a sole instructor, but we work as a family, and people say, "you've got a smashing atmosphere," explained Jodie. So while the girls teach the dances how do Mum and Dad help out? "They take the money! joked Jodie. In fact, Nobby transports the equipment for Jodie's Country, driving a Chevrolet Lumina towing a custom-built trailer.

Also as a family we all went six or eight times to

Jodie in later years with her shorter hair

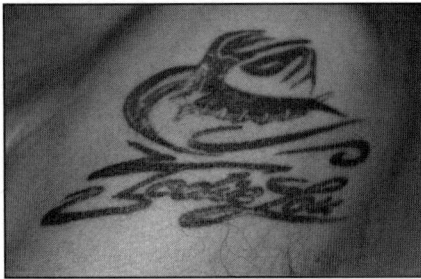

Nobby's tattoo in memory of Jodie Lou

Fan Fare in Nashville. By far Jodie's favourite country singer was Alan Jackson. She always went to his show restaurant in Pigeon Forge and we all loved Dollywood. Also she loved the Fireflys seen for the first time at night in Gatlinburg. Her other must which Jodie had to do was to go and watch the NASCARS at Nashville Speedway. Whilst in Nashville she met many stars including Ken Melons and LeAnn Rimes. One of her ambitions was to go to the Richard Petty school and do a NASCAR Driving Course. She was determined that she would do this.

During her short life she would always want to drive as from the age of six I used to let her drive the truck and trailer (sitting on my lap of course) from the entrance of S.P.R. to the pit bay. She was able to make the tight turns swinging wide and watching the trailer in the rear view mirrors.

When she was about twelve I would take her to my place of work at Allied Con. Equip. Co. Ramsden Heath where I did subcontract repairs on construction equipment. This invariably meant unsociable hours and working weekends. Whilst I was working Jodie could drive my pick up round the yard doing all the driving manoeuvres, i.e. reversing etc. The yard there was about one hundred yards long. One Sunday evening I was driving back home around the M25 with Jodie and we ran out of gas. I used to cover one hundred and fifty miles per round trip per day working and knew precisely when to fill the tank. Checking the milometer, I could not believe she had covered twenty eight miles in a yard that was only one hundred yards long. I guess she had to learn to drive, she did pass her driving test five weeks after her 17th birthday so it was worth it. Her first car was a Ford Escort, then a Ford Mondeo. I supposed it had to happen that her third car was a Pontiac Firebird which she loved, she had this when she was twenty.

In 1998 I had a very serious industrial accident I was unconscious for two or three weeks in intensive care. Whilst I was in hospital Jodie put a tape player beside my ear and played country music, mainly George Jones, my country singing idle. I don't need that rocking chair!

Because I was out of it for quite a long time Jodie would then take my Chevy pick-up for a run up the road and back and keep it very clean. I was proud of her for doing this for me when I couldn't. I was off work for nearly four years during this time and Jodie found herself a couple of jobs full time while still teaching people to line dance and then she got herself a driving job. Also at this time with my recuperation well under way (even with 12 titanium bars and 32 screws in my rebuilt face), I decided to build myself a new funny car. As Jodie was an average size I decided to build the chassis around her and she spent many hours with me setting up the steering and the controls, apart from the car she had booked herself an HGV course so that she was set up to drive the new rig everywhere as she realised I was going to need one again.

Also about this time she decided she wanted a dog so off she went and bought for herself a doberman puppy. This presented a little problem in choosing a name. Her and sister Katie took about seven days (when we just called it dog) to decide, then it happened, Jodie being a totally devoted fan of the Dukes of Hazard programme thought of the name Rosco. So he was registered with the Kennel Club, Rosco P. Coltrane – I can only say my influence

Jodie's Pontiac Firebird – her pride and joy

Above: Jodie's Pontiac Firebird and below George Jones Country Legend, autographing Jodie's hat

Rosco the Doberman

*Memorial garden and seat
dedicated to the memory of
Jodie in front of the office block
where she last worked*

must have been indirect.

Tragically my Jodie Lou's life was brought to an abrupt end on 7th April 2004 as the result of a road accident. She was just twenty four years old.

*When God comes and gathers his Jewels
All treasures and diamonds and gold
I'll meet her up there in Heaven so fair
When God comes and gathers his Jewels*

Hank Williams 1947.

Jodie and the singing cowboy in music row in Nashville

NOBBY'S QUARTER MILE

Another poem was written in memory of Jodie:

Jodie Hills ...

If you wanted to know Jodie,
then the Deep South's where you'd go,
Where "Boss Hogg" and two brothers
made the Dukes of Hazard show,
Which gave her so much pleasure,
going down her memory lane,
Where the shade of the Magnolia trees
can take away life's pain.
Where Cadillacs and pick up trucks
can park up side by side,
Where cowboys take on Broncos
in fantastic rodeo rides,
And Dancers in their cowboy boots
are formed up in a square,
Stepping backwards, sideways forwards,
Jodie Hills could take you there.
The Deep South's where her heart was,
and no doubt it's there still
Line dancing with a multitude will ever be her thrill
Teaching others what the steps are,
keeping to the music's time,
Calling out the steps to make
or leading them in mime.
Dressed in a proper outfit, yep
The Cowgirl's proper wear,
Just listen for a noisy barn,
Jodie's spirit lives on there.
Just remember all the good times,
the smiles, the laughs, the show,
Remember her for what she was,
that's what she'd want you know.

Jodie Lou

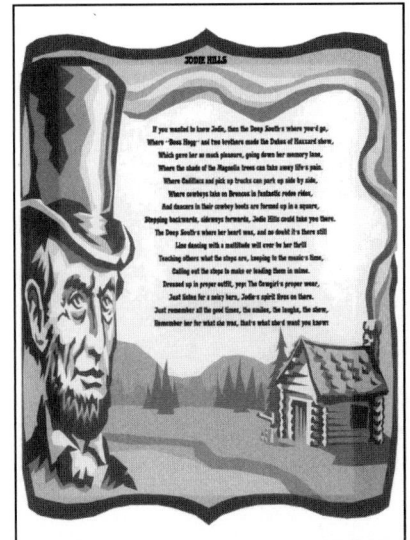

This poem has been written by the Rev. David Bradley who dedicated it to the memory of Jodie.

The Song recording ... Jodie Lou

by Paul Ansell with Scotty Moore (of Elvis fame)

I knew nothing about this very special tribute to my Jodie Lou until I was sent a copy of the CD by Paul Ansell.

It was by far the worst time of my life when Jodie was killed on the motorway. I did not know how to face the next minute of living but somehow with the support of Anne and Katie Jo I was helped through this period, and about six weeks later a CD called Paul Ansell in Memphis was delivered to me. I was informed that there was a track called Jodie Lou on it which I should listen to. This I did, under the circumstances the result was that I broke down with emotion and wondered how anyone could put together something so good to music like this, I now realise just how wonderful this was.

It seems that Paul Ansell had a request from a DJ called Tim to write a song about Jodie Lou. I think initially he was not sure what to do as he had never met her.

Having then been given lots of history about her way of life he felt that there was a song there somewhere. He had found out she loved country music, taught country line dancing, loved cars, idolised her family and lived life to the full. Tim deserves credit too for the track. Paul then got together with his guitar player and went over the track he had then written called Jodie Lou. This worked out fine because Paul and his band (Paul Ansell No. 9) were just about to fly to Memphis to record an album at Sam Phillips Sun Recording Studio in Memphis with Elvis's first and best lead guitarist Scotty Moore. How much of a coincidence is this with my love of Elvis and the fact I called my cars Houndog after the King's record of the same name.

So off they went and arrived at the studio where they were soon joined by Scotty Moore. Having recorded a couple of tracks, Paul thought let's try Jodie Lou on the third cut with Scotty Moore helping get the tempo correct, it was a take. Scotty actually plays lead guitar on the track and commented that it was his favourite so far with Paul's band.

A little bit of history in the making which made me feel a lot better.

Here is a part of the p.s. on the note that Paul sent to me after I had tracked him down to thank him:

P.s. of course when you finally tracked me down and told me how happy it had made you feel, that was the payment I was not really expecting. That was the gift out of tragedy that I never dreamt of.

Now I have met you and your lovely family, I can say for me it has been the most rewarding musical thing I have ever done.

Rewarding, not in any other way other than soulfully rewarding. To have been allowed a glimpse into your sorrow, and to me that was my privilege.

Keep rockin' ole chap and keep up the good work. Paul x

The Words of the Song:

Jodie Lou by Paul Ansell

Let me tell you something bout Jodie Lou
She could do everything that her daddy taught
her to
And her mamma will never be the same
In their hearts she lovingly remains.

Let me tell you something bout Jodie Lou
She could dance real good to a country blue
Everytime we play a different tune
Dancing somewhere you can find Jodie Lou

We're missing you what can we do
We're gonna celebrate the joy you gave Jodie Lou

Jodie-Lou got taken way before her time
Though she lived this life with passion and a smile
Things ol never be the same
Those that knew her best won't forget her name.

Missing you what can we do
We're gonna celebrate the joy you gave Jodie Lou
Missing you what can we do.
We're gonna celebrate the joy you gave Jodie Lou
We're gonna celebrate the joy you gave Jodie Lou

Jodie Lou   Jodie Lou

Paul has a DVD out now which features Jodie
Lou.

My court case

8 years after the accident (2006) ...

During my time away from working I realised that I should claim compensation for my horrific accident and the distress it had caused. This was made very difficult as the company involved were not very honest and said that I was not doing a job for them but that I had borrowed their workshop to do the work for someone else.

What came about in the end was that they had forgotten the police who had covered the accident and in the police statement they had told them that they had asked me to go there and do the job for themselves.

During the court procedure the same people queried as to how I could build a drag racing car as I had been doing and also claim compensation from themselves. They arranged for a neurologist to examine me in London. I was with him for three and a half hours and he was very thorough going through all the statements, and my drag racing life. He eventually asked me if the people that were saying I should not build a race car had any medical qualifications. I told him not to my knowledge and enquired why he had asked this. He then answered me with, "do you know Mr. Hills building this new car is the best thing you could do to help you get back to normal and I will be only too pleased to go to the court and tell them this also." I could not believe my ears anyway the compensation offer was put up in 14 days by five figures! This was nearly eight years after the accident!

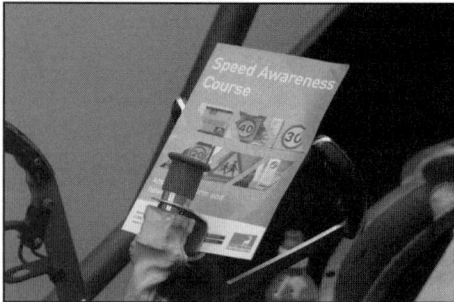

Speed awareness

A learning curve

During my research for this book and the B17 history I visited Duxford aircraft museum mainly to photograph the B17s there and also the wall that was removed from Podington Airfield was put on show there. Duxford was a very interesting place for me giving me access to the original artists paintings on the wall.

After this visit on the way home as far as Neesworth and I lifted my foot off the gas pedal as I passed the 30mph sign, unfortunately not quick enough and two weeks later I had notification that I had been recorded at 36mph. Oh dear, further correspondence and I was offered to pay a fixed penalty of £60 and three points on my licence or alternatively go on a speed awareness for £100 and if I was satisfactory on this course I would not have any points added to my licence, so I opted for this course with an open mind as I did not know what to expect at all.

I attended this course a few weeks ago. On checking in about half an hour early I was given a cup of coffee and seated at a desk in a conference room. Eventually about another twenty people arrived and the tutors Mark and Matt introduced themselves in a very professional manner and proceeded to explain how necessary it is to be aware of speed and the measure the law has of trying to ensure that all drivers are aware of the speed limits, road signs, markings and the meanings of them, etc. I found this extremely interesting, I suppose like most average people I was not as aware as I should be of the most up to date signs. It was of course about fifty three years since I passed my driving test!

During the first session the subject of stopping distance was discussed this went from 30mph to 100mph on the motorway.

I felt that I might be able to help on the 100mph stopping distance because I know travelling at a consistent 100mph over a measured ¼ mile takes exactly nine seconds, so I figured that a consistent 100mph over 110 yards takes 2¼ seconds. During the morning coffee break I put this to the tutors saying it may be a more helpful way of explaining to people how difficult it is to stop from 100mph. They agreed and asked if I would be willing to stand up and explain this. So in the next session I did this and it went down very well, of course I drew a little bit from my favourite subject in Houndog drag racing, I could have gone on for hours but I didn't, I kept it short and sweet.

I'll sum up by saying this was an excellent course and I learnt an awful lot. I think every driver should go on one of these courses every ten years after passing their driving test and also go drag racing!

Note left for Nobby from Mark Dowding – Advanced Driving Instructor:

Just wanted to drop you a short note to thank you for your professional insights you were able to share with the group on the Speed Awareness Course at the Ramada Jarvis, this Thursday just gone. It always helps us as trainers to get the message across to the public.

Many thanks and best wishes,

Mark

Nobby starting up the new car.

*Simon Hayward the driver of
the new car*

New Car Houndog 12

Update

It is now January 2008 and last year John Force had his horrific accident and dramatic safety chassis modifications need doing. I think another one hundred extra hours of welding and cutting are now needed for safety's sake. I understand these need to be done. The SFI chassis inspection was completed in February and has passed, the fly wheel, clutch, clutch can and the wheels have to be inspected so I will keep my fingers crossed.

I am now looking forward to the future and what it brings.

My last comment: most things seemed to say I should have gone on that day in December 1998, well I didn't – I'll sum it up like this:

I arrived at the Pearly Gates and here was St. Peter, cowboy boots and hat too. He looked at me and said "you ain't coming in here boy", I said "why?" He replied, "cos you ain't come in your Silverado Pick Up Truck!"

THE END

Nobby

P.S.
Fast cars and country music is what I love. Yes I do wear my jeans stacked!

Over the years I've met some real knuckle draggers. They were so very good at it. I am certain they know who they are. Fortunately there are plenty of bananas for them to feed on.

and finally ...

As a finale I must say I have visited so many places in the world and have raced or demonstrated my car at the following places to name a few:

Silverstone, Blackbushe, Gravely, Duxford, Santa Pod, Piccadilly Underpass, Gavlar in Sweden, RAF Hullavington, Aire in Scotland, Mantorp Park in Sweden, Zandvorrt in Holland, Österreich Ring in Austria, Geblestad in Switzerland, Hockenheim Ring in Germany, York Raceway, Brands Hatch, Aintree Racecourse, Crystal Palace, Donnington Park, Snetterton, HMS Daedulus, Brighton Speed Trials, Pebble Mill at Birmingham, Shakespeare County Raceway and Deepenik in Belgium not bad for a 28 year old country boy!!!!

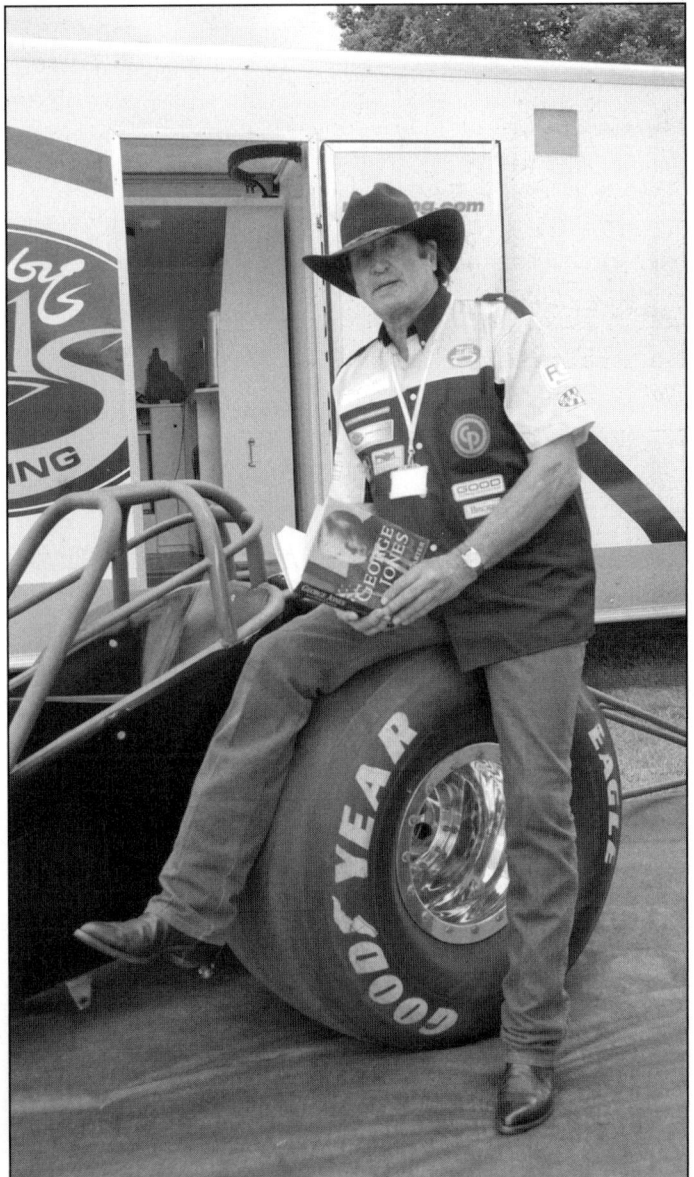

Nobby 2007 at Sandringham, Norfolk with the new Houndog 12

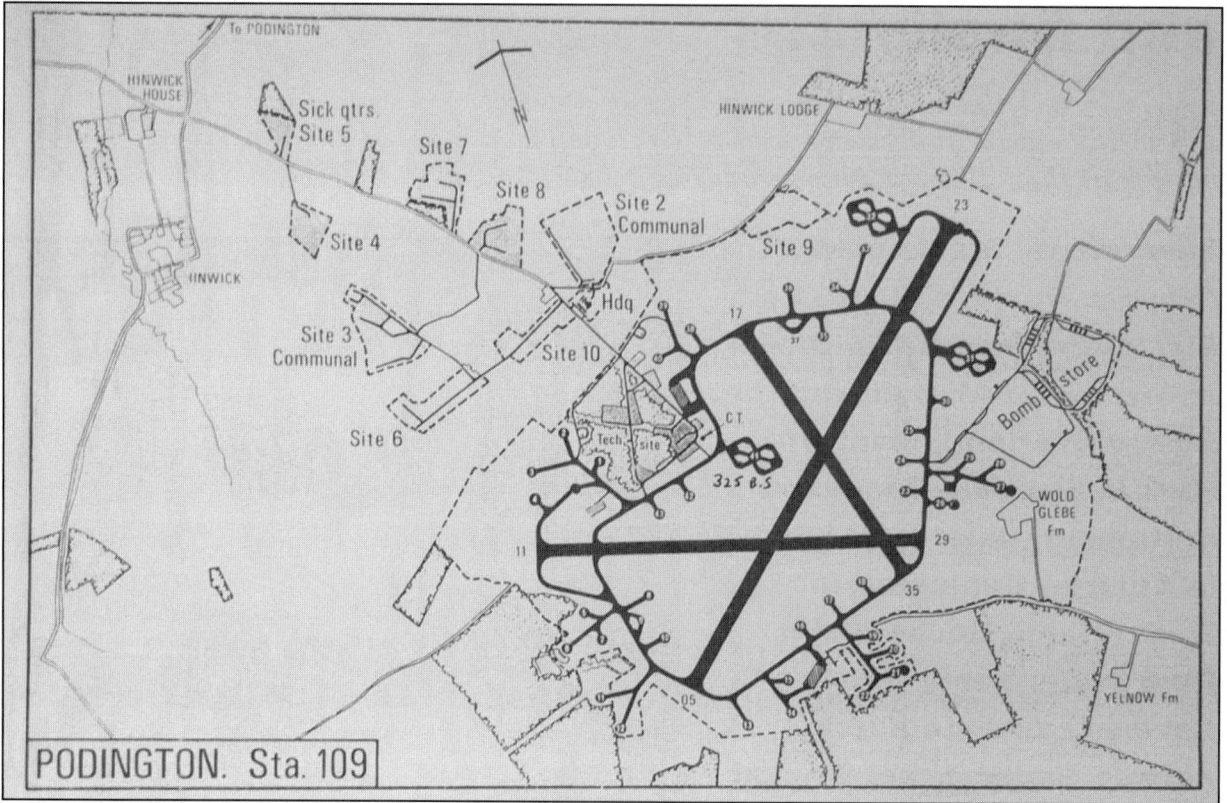

Map of Podington Airfield 1944

starting with ....

Houndog 1

Les Hill the very first Houndog driver (no relation to Nobby no s on name!)

NOBBY'S QUARTER MILE

Houndog 2

Houndog 3

Houndog 4

Houndog 5

Mike Hutcherson first drove the Houndog 3

Houndog 6

Houndog 7

Houndog 8

Houndog 9

Houndog 10

Houndog 11

and finally to 2008 and the

Houndog 12

To sum it all up:

Nobby Hills

- a poem written by Diane King 2008

As the big man walks into the room
A gentle giant comes to mind
With a love for country music
He is sensitive and kind
He doesn't think he's worthy
Of all the fuss and attention
But there's a few things about him
That are well worth a mention
The cars he's built over the years
They are his pride and joy
The way he talks about them
Is like an excited little boy
His love and dedication
Through the hardship and the strife
Racing and putting cars together
Has been a big part of his life
The awful accident that he had
Caused a lot of pain
But with the patience of lots of people
They helped build his life again
His love for Anne and Katie
And dear Jodie, who's missed a lot
She was loved by everybody
And will never be forgot
Now a book about his life
Packed so full of thrills
His friends and family all agree
He's the one and only NOBBY HILLS.